C.B. Collett

A Competent Successor

by
John Chacksfield
FBIS, MRAeS, AFAIAA, C. Eng

THE OAKWOOD PRESS

British Library Cataloguing in Publication Data
A Record for this book is available from the British Library
ISBN 0 85361 586 1

Typeset by Oakwood Graphics.
Repro by Ford Graphics, Ringwood, Hants.
Printed by Inkon Printers Ltd, Yateley, Hants.

Swindon Works on 8th September, 1935. 2-6-2T No. 4108 is under construction.
R.S. Carpenter Collection

Front cover, top: C.B. Collett.   STEAM: *Museum of the Great Western Railway*
Front cover, bottom: A contemporary postcard view of No. 4073 *Caerphilly Castle.*
John Alsop Collection
Rear cover, top: No. 5000 *Launceston Castle* at the head of the 'Cheltenham Flyer', a train which averaged 71.3 mph between Paddington and Swindon.   *John Alsop Collection*
Rear cover, bottom: A Tuck's postcard of the 'Cornish Riviera Express' with No. 6008 *King James II.*   *John Alsop Collection*

Title page: No. 6003 *King George IV* nears Reading (West) with the down 'Cornish Riviera Express' which is comprised of largely 'Centenary' stock created by Collett for this and other prime expresses to the West of England.   *John Scott-Morgan Collection*

Published by The Oakwood Press (Usk), P.O. Box 13, Usk, Mon., NP15 1YS.
E-mail: oakwood-press@dial.pipex.com
Website: www.oakwood-press.dial.pipex.com

Contents

Foreword

Although literally hundreds of books and magazine articles have been written on the Great Western locomotives designed by C.B. Collett, little has been said about the man. For someone who occupied the onerous position of Chief Mechanical Engineer (CME) of the GWR, a post held by such giants as Daniel Gooch, William Dean and George Jackson Churchward, few writers have attempted to get behind the façade created by this job.

Indeed, perhaps the biggest task for Collett to achieve was to overcome the legacy of his predecessors, most particularly his immediate predecessor G.J. Churchward, whose achievements cast a long shadow over Collett's reign as CME. There has been much debate amongst railway historians as to whether Collett merely copied and refined Churchward designs, but this book should confirm once and for all that he was his 'own man', more than capable of creating locomotive designs which were far more than carbon copies of his predecessor's ideas.

The roll call of Collett designs reads like a veritable 'Who's Who' of locomotive design and excellence - the 'Kings', 'Castles', 'Halls', 'Manors' and 'Granges' were the mainstay of the GWR locomotive fleet, and examples of most of these classes still grace our preserved railways and museums today - indeed our museum has perhaps two of the most famous of all, the pioneering No. 6000 *King George V* and No. 4073 *Caerphilly Castle*.

Whilst the evidence for Collett's design genius still survives in locomotives still running today, this biography fills in the gap for the other aspect of the man, his character and personality. Events in his life, particularly the loss of his wife played an important part in shaping the development of his career, and John Chacksfield has been able to give a well rounded portrait of a man who until now has been something of an unknown quantity to those who did not work with or for him. With the publication of this book, another chapter of Great Western history has been written, and the contribution of a man who did so much to further the success of the company he worked for , has been finally recognised.

Tim Bryan
Curator
STEAM: Museum of the Great Western Railway
Swindon
Wilts
February 2002

Preamble

Charles Collett was, initially, a difficult subject to cover, yet I felt that his time as Chief Mechanical Engineer of the Great Western Railway (GWR) should be recorded in the context of his personal life, should enough information be forthcoming. Collett had no descendants and it was only late in my researches that some family information surfaced. However, some people who worked with him have put pen to paper and from their writings I was able to gather some measure of assessment as to his character, the way he thought and, by reference to his locomotives, a fair appreciation of his design philosophy.

The far-seeing strategy of G.J. Churchward was the foundation of Collett's design programme and his involvement as Assistant Works Manager and then Works Manager during the commencement of the standard locomotive production, gave him a clear insight into the background to the steady development of the baseline designs, which he continued from his accession to the position of CME in 1922.

A very private, deep-thinking person, Collett sometimes could, by his attitude, be thought of as an aloof character, and had his wife, to whom he was devoted, not died when she did, his two decades as CME might have been even greater than they undoubtedly were. However, as the book implies, one of his technical advances was most certainly ahead of many other railways, this being the drive to introduce diesel units for passenger services, a development which was unfortunately curtailed by the advent of World War II and the lack of adequate profits to allow the necessary investment for a more complete programme.

His involvement in the metaphysical ways became somewhat of an obsession in his later years, but the engineering expertise was not dimmed by such diversions in his private life, as witness the large number of his designs which are preserved and serve on the many privately run railways throughout the UK.

Here then, is the story of how Charles Collett achieved the top engineering position on the GWR and made his name as a notable locomotive creator for that railway.

C.B. Collett. Portrait taken about 1922.   *STEAM: Museum of the Great Western Railway*

Introduction and Acknowledgements

Having myself covered Maunsell, Fowler and Stanier in biographies, and with Gresley and Bulleid being well-documented elsewhere, the possibility of covering Collett raised its head. I felt that, should this prove feasible, then at last all the major CMEs of the post-Grouping era would have been described in biographical form. The completion of this task, then, is contained herein and it is hoped that one more gap in a biography list has been plugged.

These engineers who rose to the pinnacle of their respective railways' engineering departments were men of great character and ability, each with his own approach to the problems associated with locomotive design, development and production. In some cases they did not ignore the precepts and principles laid down by those before them. Collett was one such engineer, who used the legacy of Churchward's expertise and planning to much good effect in his 19½ years in office. His interpretation of the needs of the Great Western Railway's motive power fleet produced some outstanding designs which were to last, in the majority of cases, through to the end of steam in the UK.

Churchward was a hard act to follow, for he had instigated a standardisation policy destined to be followed to the final days of the Great Western Railway as a public company and, subsequently, the Western Region of British Railways (BR). He was also notable for his adoption of design features likely to improve the performance and economy of the steam locomotive. His research into locomotive design, viz the adoption of long lap, long travel valve gear, coupled to much care in the design of the boilers was legendary, with many of the precepts being eventually adopted on the other railways.

C.B. Collett, having been Works Manager and Principal Assistant to Churchward through many of the above developments, was ideally placed to take charge when Churchward retired at the end of 1921 and made an impact almost immediately with his 'Castle' class 4-6-0, as he continued to design in his predecessor's way, safe in the knowledge that he was following the philosophy of, perhaps, the greatest British locomotive engineer of all time, and certainly of the 20th century.

The analysis of a complex personality such as Charles Collett has been a central theme throughout this book. Those who knew Collett have long departed this life and so some theories, if they seem acceptable, are speculative. I have endeavoured to be as fair as possible to a sometimes shadowy person. Certainly his predecessor, Churchward, due to his involvement with both the workforce and the local community, has been recorded very faithfully as a great engineer who selected Collett as a worthy successor. Whether he had hoped this very capable production engineer would come out of his shell and prosper as a competent CME, much involved in Works and local matters cannot be gauged, but it is thought that this may have been the case. Churchward's judgement in this context was slightly flawed, as we shall see. However, Charles Collett, if deficient in the outgoing sense, most certainly was capable of coming up with balanced arguments to promote the design programme he instituted and clearly was held in some esteem by the GWR Board. Had they wished, they could have engineered his removal from office. However, his immediate deputy in the latter years, John Auld, was older than himself and therefore not a candidate. This is just one small hint of some deviousness in Collett who, throughout his CME incumbency acquired a reputation for such behaviour amongst those who had limited, or no, contact with him.

Much has been written by many authors about the locomotives attributed to both Churchward and Collett, but little about the latter engineer's personal life and background. All too often we find that Churchward takes the credit for many designs to emerge from the 1922-41 era when Collett was CME. Collett, however, was an extremely competent production engineer who was responsible for the eclipse of the smaller express engines on the GWR, replacing them with larger, more versatile, types to cope with the increasing train loads of the 1920s and 1930s. He also instigated the widespread use of the diesel railcar on the lightly used, but important, cross-country services in the second decade of his time as CME. On the production side, he had the vast facilities of the Swindon works at his beck and call and, even despite that, the productive capacity of these premises needed supplementing by some outside contractors at one particular period. From these works and the private builders came the hundreds of locomotives that typified the 'Great' in the GWR. For great they were, both in technical features and operating economy, such that a large number have been rescued from scrapyards and, following dedicated rebuilding, still serve on many of the preserved steam railways as a fine testimony to Churchward and Collett.

Today, the great works at Swindon are largely gone and the site is now a conglomeration of shops and industrial undertakings and, of course, the new GWR museum 'STEAM', formerly sited in the town across the main line. This town, the newer part born by the need to house the workforce required by the GWR plant, has moved into the modern age, but one still connects it to those halcyon days when the railway reigned supreme as the main means of transport throughout the UK.

The task of delving into the life of Charles Collett has not been easy, but assistance has come from many directions. I am deeply grateful to Mrs Margaret Chadd (née Collett) for her generous response to my queries on her family research resulting in her book *The Collett Saga*, from which I have been able to trace the origin of the family in England. The libraries of both the Institution of Mechanical Engineers and Institution of Civil Engineers dug into their respective archives for me. Collett's old school, Merchant Taylors, provided the limited educational and family data as still exists from their records. The Great Western Railway Museum at Swindon was most helpful, providing access to its extensive photographic collection and the GWR Locomotive Committee minutes, copies of which they hold. George Carpenter, as usual, produced contacts which enabled an insight into Swindon practices to be assessed.

Individual help has also come from members of the Friends of the Great Western Museum, including Jack Willcock who provided information concerning Collett's successor, F.W. Hawksworth. Much help was also proffered by Swindon Reference Library. The library of the Royal Aeronautical Society furnished the information on the Railway Air Services covered in Chapter Ten.

As with all books of this kind, the illustrations are important as many show the results of design studies under the control of the subject. I am again indebted to John Scott-Morgan for letting me have free run of his extensive GWR collection, many of which are on carefully preserved glass slides, and have not been published before. Roger Carpenter also supplied a considerable batch of relevant photos spanning the whole of Collett's lifetime.

Chapter One

Collett, The Early Years

English literature had recently lost the genius of Charles Dickens, whose writings were soon to be reckoned as classics. But the literary field still flourished in 1871 with the publication of George Eliot's *Middlemarch*. In the engineering field, the Royal Navy had nearly completed the switch from now outdated sail to steam, whilst on the railways, F.W. Webb had taken charge at the LNWR Crewe works and commenced an illustrious career there. At Swindon, Joseph Armstrong was building a range of four-coupled, broad gauge, express locomotives to supplement those of Gooch. The Great Western Railway was prospering as never before, with its broad gauge of 7 ft 0¼ in. seemingly set to continue for all time, although rumblings of discontent were being heard at places of transfer to the standard gauge. Some mixed gauge track had already appeared at Paddington where the GWR shared tracks with the Metropolitan Railway, but another 21 years were to elapse before Brunel's legacy was to disappear forever. It was also two years before George Jackson Churchward was taken on as a pupil of John Wright at the Newton Abbot works of the South Devon Railway.

It was in this year that Charles Benjamin Collett was born. The Colletts are now a large and varied family throughout the UK, its Commonwealth and many other countries. The name itself can be traced back to Norman origins, as a Colet was recorded on one of the copies of the Roll of Battle Abbey. This reference appears as one Jean Colet, Sieur de Bernonville. Even before the Conquest there were Colets in Rouen trading with England. Around the 13th century the spelling of the name begins to change to Collett and the descendants of these Norman traders and invaders were, by then, well established as Lords of Manors and clergy.

The lineage of interest in this biography is that established in Gloucestershire, of which a Thomas Collett (d.1538) and his wife Alice produced seven children; William, Henry, John, Elizabeth, Joan, Alice and Agnes. Of this line John is the person of interest. John's third son Henry, born in 1555, was to have nine children. Thomas, the eldest son of Henry only had one boy, named Thomas after his father.

This Thomas and his wife Hannah had four children, Thomas, Joseph, John and Hester. Joseph entered the clergy and married a Hannah Williams. Their eldest son Joseph's fourth son, Ebenezer, became the Member of Parliament for Cashel in 1819. Ebenezer was the great-grandfather of our subject. Politics became a profession for his eldest son John, who was elected as MP for Athlone.

Ebenezer's youngest son Benjamin, born in 1812, married a Charlotte Sampson and lived at Grafton Manor, Worcestershire. They had seven children, three girls, Harriett, Margaret and Charlotte, and four boys, Charles Benjamin, John, William and Thomas Clay.

Of these, William, a journalist by profession, married Mary Helen Cooke in 1867 and continued to live at Grafton Manor. They were to have just two sons,

A Gooch design of 1851, this 0-6-0 *Flirt* would have been in service when Collett was born. The appearance of a camera certainly attracts the shed staff!   *R.S. Carpenter Collection*

A view familiar to young Collett, the down 'Zulu' passing Ealing 18th August, 1890. A 'Rover' class 4-2-2 at the head.   *R.S. Carpenter Collection*

William, born in 1869 and Charles Benjamin, our subject, born on the 10th September, 1871. Charles only knew his elder brother for eight years, for William died at the age of ten.

Grafton Manor was to be Charles' home for a few childhood years, and his first sight of a steam locomotive would have been on the railway feature of note nearby, this being the Lickey Incline which starts its 1 in 37½ climb from Bromsgrove station, which lies just two miles from the Manor. He and his brother would have heard the sound of hard-worked engines taking their trains up this fearsome bank on a daily basis, particularly on quiet evenings with a north-easterly breeze blowing.

Grafton Manor still stands and functions as a high-class hotel and is recognised as one of Worcestershire's great historic houses. Established before the Norman Conquest, the present Manor has been considerably rebuilt following a disastrous fire in the 1700s. It boasts a 15th century private chapel and is surrounded by 26 acres of well-kept grounds.

Charles' early years were spent at Grafton Manor until a move came, to London, where the family set up home at No. 33, Tavistock Crescent, Westbourne Park. The change from a country life to the suburbs, as they were in those days, of London was tempered by the proximity of nearby bustle at the Great Western Railway's engine shed at Westbourne Park.

Charles Benjamin was to become very much a key employee of the GWR in later years as he advanced through the ranks to the top. His second home was a stone's throw from the GWR main line out of Paddington. No. 33, Tavistock Crescent has, with most of the other properties in that road, long been swept away by redevelopment. It backed onto the Metropolitan line (now the Hammersmith and City line), the other side of which lay the Westbourne Park Shed. This, up to 1906, was the main shed in the Paddington area. From the upstairs back windows of his home young Charles would have watched the collection of broad gauge locomotives coming and leaving on their duties. The air would have been full of smoke and steam, and the noise of engines moving about during their replenishment and inspection periods on shed. He also would have watched the arrivals and departures of the smartly turned out broad gauge expresses passing along the main line just the other side of the shed and sidings.

Just how much this may have influenced him in his eventual choice of career can only be surmised, but many small boys, through the past 150 years, have been stirred to consider a railway or engineering career by the sight of steam locomotives or their diesel successors thundering by with their trains.

Charles' early education was probably largely at home, his father, still practising as a journalist, was clearly a gentleman of the upper middle class. And so it was, at the age of 10, he started his formal education at Merchant Taylors' School, then located at Charterhouse Square, on the fringe of the City of London. Some of Charles' forebears are recorded as pupils of this long-established school, as far back as 1568 and, in fact, he was the slightly junior of the two Colletts attending from 1882. The elder remained at the school for a further two years after Charles left and then obtained a scholarship to St John's College, Oxford. Not far from the school was Farringdon Street station, to which

Charles Collett's birthplace and childhood home, Grafton Manor, near Bromsgrove.   *Author*

No. 33 Tavistock Crescent is now the site of a modern development of apartments. In the right background can be seen Westbourne Park station.   *Author*

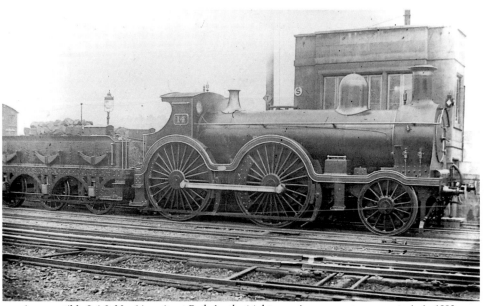

A convertible 2-4-0, No. 14, waits at Bath for the 'right away' on an up passenger train in 1890.
R.S. Carpenter Collection

No. 14 is found at speed near Bath in 1892. The scene is a wintery one, and would therefore be a few months before the broad gauge was to be erased for ever. *R.S. Carpenter Collection*

GWR broad gauge trains ran over the Metropolitan, which had agreed to the mixed gauge track in return for GWR contributions towards the connection at Paddington. Charles would probably have travelled to school via the Metropolitan trains over this line whilst the family lived in Westbourne Park, whose station was just a few yards around the corner from their home.

A great loss came in 1884, when his father died quite suddenly, clearly leaving his mother adequately well off, for his education at Merchant Taylors continued.

Charles Collett spent six years as a pupil at Merchant Taylors, gathering his education, where he showed promise in Mathematics and such Science as there was in those days, for in 1887 he was taken on as an apprentice at the eminent firm of Marine Engineers, Messrs Maudslay, Sons and Field, Ltd. Some reports have him as a pupil of Joshua Field, but this would not be possible as that eminent engineer died in the 1860s. However, this apprenticeship was a crucial part of Charles' training. That company was, perhaps, the leader in marine engine design and construction throughout the mid-1800s. Henry Maudslay and Joshua Field, the firm's founders, were top-class engineers who placed great emphasis on perfection in their products. The company, in its early days, had been involved in the supply of boilers and engines for Brunel's steamship, the *Great Eastern*. It also had produced some of the pumping equipment for the ill-fated South Devon atmospheric railway promoted by the same great engineer. Maudslay's had no experience in operating their products and the training available with them would have had a strong production bias. Collett's main attributes in quality and production engineering clearly came from these early days and were to be of great benefit to the GWR in his later years.

A down express speeds past Acton with a 'Rover' class 4-2-2 *Great Western* in charge. This 'rebuild' incorporated some components of the first locomotive to be built at Swindon (originally as a 2-2-2) in 1846.   *R.S. Carpenter Collection*

His theoretical engineering education was satisfied by attendance at the City and Guilds Engineering College in South Kensington (now part of Imperial College) during this apprenticeship. There is, however, no record of any degree being conferred. Collett never acknowledged one in any documentation lodged at the I.Mech.E. or I.Civil E. Notwithstanding this, it is clear from his subsequent career that considerable engineering knowledge was acquired from his attendance at the College.

In 1893, at the termination of his time with Maudslay's, Collett was very fortunate to be offered an engineering post on the GWR, at its Swindon works. This in itself was an unusual step, for the railway did not often take on outsiders in the technical offices, preferring to supply the staff from its own apprentices and pupils or, occasionally, other railways' drawing offices. However, as engineers trained at Maudslay's were known within the engineering industries as 'Men of Maudslays' this fact may well have been one part of the events which sufficed for Collett to be considered for employment. So, clearly, his railway engineering knowledge was picked up from this time onwards. He was to prove a good learner in that context.

The happenings leading up to Collett's obtaining the draughtsman's post at Swindon have never been revealed, but after inspection of the family tree the following scenario is postulated as a possible chain of events.

Collett's uncle John, on his father's side, was Director of Naval Contracts, which would have brought him into close contact with a wide range of companies providing equipment for Royal Navy vessels. On such company was Maudslay's, which we have seen was a leading producer of marine and specialist steam engines. It is logical to speculate that uncle John's suggestions and influence led to the apprenticeship at Maudslay's for his nephew. Clearly, all the time he was undergoing this training, Collett still harboured a great interest in railway locomotives, an interest fired by his boyhood days near the Westbourne Park Shed operations. This was communicated to his uncle who, in his top Civil Service position would have had membership of one, or possibly more, of the London Clubs. Top officials of the GWR, in particular the Directors, would also be found in these Clubs. Some conversations between John Collett and one of them may well have resulted in a quiet word being put Dean's way, probably after a Board meeting, about this young man with an engineering bent who still hankered after steam locomotives. A bright young man, with a Maudslay's training, who could be a useful addition to the design office.

From this speculative analysis one detects a determination by Collett not to be diverted from his early thoughts of involvement with railway locomotives. He was, in later years, well-known for his single-minded ways and determination to carry out his responsibilities in a manner acceptable to his philosophies.

The broad gauge had disappeared the previous year, but the yards at Swindon were still full of withdrawn locomotives and stock awaiting scrapping or conversion to standard gauge. The position Collett was offered was as a draughtsman. The drawing offices were located in a building, situated in the neck of the junction between the Bristol and Gloucester lines, dating from 1842 and first modified in 1870. It was L-shaped in plan and comprised the eastern extension of the original works. We are not certain where Collett found lodgings after obtaining

William Dean, the experimenter and reluctant retiree.
STEAM: Museum of the Great Western Railway

his position a Swindon, it is thought that he took rooms in Bath Street. This was conveniently close to the works entrance at the north end of Emlyn Square.

The entry of Charles Collett into the drawing office from an outside position would have been viewed with some degree of coolness by the established staff. His normal reticence to engage in much general conversation must have engendered a degree of caution in those who had to approach him. By 1895 both Dean and Churchward, the newly appointed Assistant Works Manager, had clearly quite quickly noted his potential and were determined to size him up on his abilities rather than personality. Collett's engineering perception clearly came across in a very positive way and, recognising this, it was planned to give him a chance to prove himself. This, if successful, was to be followed by a move to a more responsible position once he had to assimilated the normal Swindon working practices in and around the design offices.

His early days were thus spent gaining experience of the many aspects covered in this large office, ending up in the civil engineering area, dealing with the building side of things. Around this time, 1894-95, he was meeting and corresponding with Ethelwyn May Simon, the daughter of the Revd Henry Simon, who was a clergyman living in the parish of Bloomsbury. Their friendship blossomed, and Charles' advancement at Swindon prospered such that they were able to contemplate marriage. The wedding took place at her parish church, St George's, Bloomsbury on 4th November, 1896. Following the honeymoon they returned to Swindon and set up their first home in Swindon. Collett's address on the wedding certificate is No. 35, Bath Terrace. Clearly, this is an error and should be Bath Street. According to local records the newly-weds set up home at No. 7, Bath Street, now renamed Bathampton Street, which is to be found in the original Railway Village of the 1860s.

Shortly after his marriage Collett was promoted and placed in charge of the Building Drawing Office. His potential was clearly being watched, for just a year later, he was promoted yet again, to assistant to the chief draughtsman.

William Dean was still nominally in command at the top in Swindon, as Locomotive, Carriage and Wagon Superintendent. However, his health, in the context of his mental capacity, was failing and, with G.J. Churchward as his Works Manager and Principal Assistant on the locomotive affairs, matters were set to slip out of his hands. This was to be a gradual process, with Churchward taking on more and more responsibility for the design aspects, without appearing to usurp the position of the much respected Dean. Clearly Churchward, in particular, recognised in Collett a future high-flyer, he was still in his mid-20s, and was prepared to give him the responsibility.

Having to deal more with the mechanical areas connected with locomotives, carriages and wagons gave Charles Collett a solid grounding for the future. In his assistant chief draughtsman role, he would have been almost entirely absorbed with that side of things, for there was a second assistant's post which dealt with more general matters such as buildings and civil engineering.

And so, by the time that Dean was being gently prepared for retirement, with Churchward taking on more and more design decisions, the position of Assistant Works Manager was to become vacant. This was the traditional route for up-and-coming youngsters to tread should they be considered for eventual promotion to high office on many, if not most, of the railways.

No 3021 *Wigmore Castle*, a Dean 4-2-2 at speed near Acton in 1900. The name was to be resurrected on the Collett 'Castle' No. 5022 of the 1932 batch.   *R.S. Carpenter Collection*

By 1910 the Dean 'Singles' were on their way out. Here No. 3031 *Achilles* is found at Worcester, still in immaculate condition.   *R.S. Carpenter Collection*

Churchward, like so many of the eminent railway engineers, had a flair for selecting young men of ability whom he reckoned would be willing enough to adopt his own ideas in practice. Charles Collett's abilities as a leading draughtsman had clearly come to his notice and, wishing to ensure that a possible successor would be well-schooled in what he was planning for the GWR locomotive policy, the promising youngster was selected to be placed under the Works Manager, H.C. King, as Assistant Works Manager. If Collett's undoubted engineering and administrative skills were used to the full, he could eventually expect to succeed King and be set for future advancement to high office.

The Works Manager's offices were located in a substantial two-storied block which had been converted in around 1889-90 from the early iron store building of 1846. This provided more spacious accommodation for the Works Manager and his by now substantial staff. The building still exists, having been preserved for use in the redevelopment of the works site. It was with this placing that Collett commenced his climb to the top.

Churchward's perception may be illustrated in his determination to apply his long stroke, long lap valve gear philosophy. He had already decided to prove his ideas by using a small stationary steam engine embodying such valve gear. With this he satisfied himself that he was able to get a much fuller opening to exhaust when the cut-off was at a low figure.

He accordingly selected Collett as Assistant Works Manager and put with him G.H. Pearson and J.W. Cross as junior assistants. This team was to carry out the experimental and development work in connection with the design and manufacture of the hardware for the experimental engine, and were to work in conjunction with George Burrows in the drawing office. It was in this manner that the great stride forward in valve gears was taken which transformed the performance and economy of all future GWR locomotives.

These early years working with Churchward had a profound effect upon Charles Collett as they did with George Pearson, who was to take the valve gear and taper boiler ideas with him when he moved to the South Eastern & Chatham Railway (SECR) as Works Manager under Maunsell in 1913. Maunsell took little persuading to adopt Swindon ideas, he could see the distinct advantages from the performance of the GWR locomotives.

The Works Manager's Office at Swindon. One of the buildings to remain virtually intact to this day.   *Author*

No. 9, London Street in 2001. Reconverted to two houses Nos. 9 and 9A. About a minute's walk to the works entrance along the street.   *Author*

Chapter Two

The Works Days

Collett's time as Assistant Works Manager of the locomotive works came at a time of great change in the locomotive design philosophy of the GWR. Up to 1897, with Dean fully in charge, the designs had been a mix of excellent and reliable types to catastrophic failures. He had been an experimenter and cost the GWR a considerable amount with unsuccessful prototypes. Much of the stock produced was distinctly Victorian in style and the introduction of new technology minimal. Dean was becoming more and more incapacitated by his years and clearly was not able to absorb the new precepts coming along. Superheating was raising its head, piston valves were emerging as a more efficient means of arranging steam distribution and exhaust and the Belpaire firebox becoming more commonplace. This last feature had been instigated on one of the last of the Dean designs in 1897, largely due to diplomatic persuasion by Churchward. Superheating and piston valves, however, had to wait until Dean had departed.

As Charles Collett settled into his new post he would have had to take stock of the rather dramatic changes taking place at Swindon as Churchward laid the foundation of a series of locomotive designs, incorporating many new concepts in the form of his adoption of American practice in styling combined with his own radical approach to production standardisation. Also he wished to carry out some research into boiler design and front end design. Indeed, the basic programme originally drawn up in 1901 for a range of standard locomotives was to be perpetuated, with subtle modifications and additions, until the demise of steam in the 1960s, such was its potential. The success of this programme meant that this would be a hard act to follow, but in future years Collett was to succeed magnificently in continuing the Churchward tradition to great effect as the GWR moved through the 1920s and 1930s towards World War II. We shall see how that happened later on.

Concurrent with the promotion came a move of home for the Colletts from Bath Street to No. 9, London Street. This was one of a row of houses built in 1845 and originally intended as four-roomed tenements but later to be converted into eight-roomed houses.

However, one of the first matters requiring the attention of Collett was the expansion programme at Swindon, which was under way from 1901. A new erecting shop, 'A' shop, was to be built in phases over the next two years and his previous experience as Head of the Building drawing office was put to good use as the Works Manager, H.C. King, required competent help in the associated reorganisation of the works. The new erecting shop was almost five acres in area and, additionally, in keeping with developments in other railway plants, electricity was to be introduced for about one-third of the machinery installed throughout the works. The supply came from an electric plant consisting of a 250 bhp Westinghouse gas engine coupled to a dynamo.

King and Collett, with their staff, organised this extensive programme, completing the new shop by 1903, in time for its use in Churchward's programme of standard locomotives production which was about to start in earnest.

French compound No. 102 *La France*, with original boiler, on a Bournemouth express of mixed GWR and LSWR stock leaves Leamington, c.1914.

R.S. Carpenter Collection

At this time, other big changes were being made to the general office block, which was increased by a further floor. This upward extension was to contain all the drawing offices. Churchward wished to have all the design disciplines under one roof to ensure that a free interchange between them was possible. The new floor was L-shaped in plan and split into three sections. The arm parallel to the Bristol line contained the locomotive, carriage and wagon sections with the chief draughtsman, chief inspector of materials and their clerks in smaller partitioned offices at the far, eastern, end. The arm to the north was the general engineering drawing office, mainly for mechanical and civil engineering, which covered such matters as cranes, hydraulics, machinery, gas, points and crossings, structural steelwork and buildings. The portion joining the two arms was a square area which was used by the planners and surveyors. This layout was to remain virtually unchanged for the remainder of Collett's time on the GWR.

As one of the great CMEs who took a personal interest in matters ongoing in the drawing office, Churchward was open to new ideas and techniques if he thought they merited incorporation. In his basic programme he originally started planning for the simplest of cylinders and motion, that is the two-cylinder layout, with the idea that this would be a standard feature regardless of usage or type. However, events surrounding the introduction of the French four-cylinder compounds had led him to develop his own four-cylinder simple designs and thereby adopt that layout for his major express locomotive developments. Additionally, the original two standard boilers were to grow into five standards for the range of design variations that appeared from the original list of six standard locomotives. Likewise, other cylinder bores and strokes and piston valve sizes were added to the baseline designs as the development programme continued. See *Table One (overleaf)* for the outline of this.

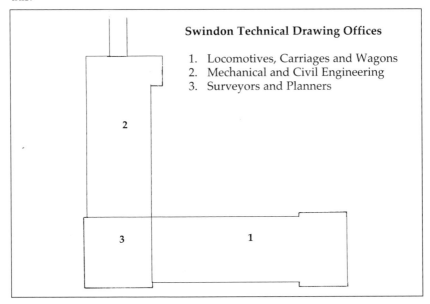

Swindon Technical Drawing Offices

1. Locomotives, Carriages and Wagons
2. Mechanical and Civil Engineering
3. Surveyors and Planners

Table One - Churchward 'Standard' Designs as initially set out in 1901

Ref. No.	1	2	3	4	5	6
Class name	'28XX'	'Manor'	'Saint'	'31XX'	'County Tank'	'County'
Type	2-8-0	4-6-0	4-6-0	2-6-2T	4-4-2T	4-4-0
Boiler Barrel length	15 ft 0 in.	15 ft 0 in.	15 ft 0 in.	11 ft 2 in.	11 ft 2 in.	11 ft 2 in.
Maximum dia.	5 ft 0 in.	5 ft 0 in.	5 ft 0 in.	5 ft 0 in.	5 ft 0 in.	5 ft 0 in.
Firebox length	9 ft 0 in.	9 ft 0 in.	9 ft 0 in.	8 ft 0 in.	8 ft 0 in.	8 ft 0 in.
Connecting rods	10 ft 8 in.	10 ft 8 in.	10 ft 8 in.	6 ft 10 in.	6 ft 10 in.	6 ft 10 in.
Driving wheels	4 ft 7 in.	5 ft 8 in.	6 ft 8 in.	5 ft 8 in.	6 ft 8 in.	6 ft 8 in.
Pony, bogie or radial wheels	3 ft 3 in.	3 ft 3 in.	3 ft 3 in.	3 ft 3 in.	3 ft 3 in.	3 ft 3 in.
Cylinders (2)						
Diameter	18 in.	18 in.	18 in.	18 in.	18 in.	18 in.
Stroke	30 in.	30 in.	30 in.	30 in.	30 in.	30 in.
Piston valve dia.	8 in.	8 in.	8 in.	8 in.	8 in.	8 in.
First built	June 1903	1936	Feb. 1902	Sept. 1903	Dec. 1905	May 1904
No. built						
(Churchward)	85	-	77	81	30	40
(Collett)	83	80	-	210	-	-

Upon the retirement of William Dean from the post of Locomotive, Carriage and Wagon Superintendent in 1902, Churchward slid effortlessly into this office. He had been expecting it and over the past two or three years had been more or less running Dean's job with great diplomacy as the great man's health was fading fast. Churchward had sufficient sensitivity such that Dean would not be aware of this, and to the great credit of the GWR Board of Directors they played along with this. Dean had been an outstanding Superintendent for nearly a quarter of a century, seeing the railway through the difficult change-over from broad gauge to standard gauge in 1892 and was much respected in the railway sphere.

This awareness of the need to be, at times, very cautious with policy matters was just one of Churchward's many attributes. As with so many eminent engineers he must look forward to those days when he himself would come to retirement and be aware of the need to have someone at hand to step into his post. Charles Collett's name was clearly noted, as he had risen from draughtsman to Assistant Works Manager in just seven years and had undoubted ability. Here was someone to be watched and encouraged as a possible successor in later years.

So often the route to the top on the locomotive side of the railways came through the Works Manager's office - it was almost a tradition that when a Locomotive Superintendent retired or moved elsewhere his place was filled by the Works Manager. There were a few isolated cases where this unwritten rule did not apply, for instance R.E.L. Maunsell got the CME post on the SE&CR from his CME post at the Inchicore works of the Great Southern & Western Railway. But then, he had, prior to the Inchicore CME job, been Works Manager there. So, as the 'standard' designs were being formulated by Churchward, we find Collett in a position whereby a future rise to Works Manager would put him in position for eventual selection as CME.

The Assistant Works Managership ensured that he would most certainly be aware, and probably involved in some, of the philosophy behind the initial designs produced as the standardisation programme took shape. The first locomotive to appear under this scheme was the two-cylinder 4-6-0 of what eventually became the '2900' or 'Saint' class. This had actually emerged from Swindon works before Dean finally retired, which is indicative of Churchward's position relative to the Board on locomotive policy matters.

Despite his lack of 'hands-on' shop-floor experiences, so far as locomotive construction went, Charles Collett clearly absorbed the necessary expertise during his early years as Assistant Works Manager, when constant visits to the various shops would have been necessary. His involvement in the setting up of the new 'A' shop as a major production centre was also of benefit, as here was a brand new production facility being formed which was to become the focus of attention for Swindon works. The vastness of this shop enabled production cycles to be planned such that manufacturing efficiency would have been much improved over the older, more cramped, shops used previously.

One further feature which Churchward was to introduce was the taper boiler, a feature to be adopted by other CMEs in later years. This resulted from his desire to achieve an ideal circulation in the boiler to effect good heat transfer and eliminate as far as possible the damage to stays through excessive local heat spots. The trouble with damaged stays led to considerable boiler maintenance costs. Collett had much to do with these boiler refinements and, keeping Pearson and Cross as key assistants, he was involved in the construction of some experimental boilers for research into circulation. It was these particular experiments that led directly to the tapered boiler, the previous baseline parallel design having restricted the flow between the barrel and the water legs of the firebox.

By the time the second 4-6-0 prototype, No. 98, was under construction, the first tapered boiler appeared with a coned rear ring, the lower portion remaining horizontal. Once refined in the area of the firebox, itself given a taper to the rear, this form of construction continued as standard practice for the majority of the future standard boilers. There were to be a few notable exceptions to this rule, for instance many of the pannier tanks had parallel boiler shells.

Much of the development work involved Collett making sure that the boiler shop had the necessary tooling to deal with the complex shapes arising from the tapers put on boiler barrels and firebox inner and outer casings. The way in which the experimental work and manufacture was accomplished quickly and efficiently by Collett and his small team was noted. The problem with stays was resolved by the careful shaping given by the circulation experiments and, although the end result was expensive to manufacture, the boiler life was increased considerably and maintenance costs thereby reduced, thus balancing the production cost increase over the anticipated life of the boiler.

Not one to launch into series production for a totally new concept without exhaustive trials, Churchward had one further prototype 4-6-0 built, No. 171, for the assessment of design improvements before inaugurating full production in 1905 and onwards. This, to become known as the 'Saint 'class, equates broadly to the reference design 3 in *Table One*.

There was an incident in May 1906 involving 'Saint' class No. 2903 *Lady of Lyons* on a trial trip from the works reportedly having attained a speed of 120 mph when running down the 1 in 300 gradient past Badminton. The story goes that someone

Churchward 2-cylinder Atlantic No. 188 at Weston-super-Mare in 1906; rebuilt as a 4-6-0 in May 1912 and assimilated into the 'Saint' class.

R.S. Carpenter Collection

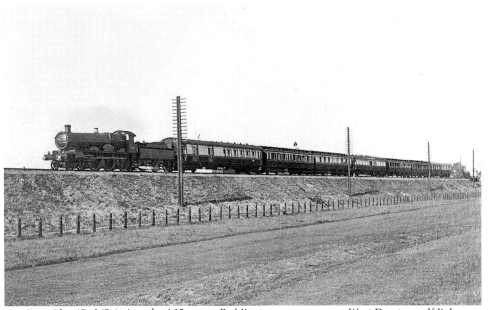

An unidentified 'Saint' on the 4.15 pm ex-Paddington express passes West Drayton golf links, 31st May, 1909.   *R.S. Carpenter Collection*

The 1906 batch of 'Saints', all ladies, included this one No. 2907 *Lady Disdain* seen at Bristol Shed in 1910.   *R.S. Carpenter Collection*

'2800' class 2-8-0 No. 2873 approaches Dainton tunnel with a substantial down freight (banker working hard at rear) in 1948-49.   *John Scott-Morgan Collection*

The Churchward 2-8-0 was to remain in production for 39 years, such was its usefulness. Here No. 2863, built in 1919, rests between duties in the mid-1930s.   *John Scott-Morgan Collection*

had suggested that one could take an engine straight from the shops and run it at a speed of 100 mph. Clearly, to some, this was a challenge to the design and manufacturing abilities of Swindon works which might be taken up as circumstances permitted. However, the account of this high speed trial was kept very much under wraps for many years. It is relevant to note those who went on this test run. Apart from Charles Collett, there was Mr G.H. Flewellen, a locomotive inspector, and Mr Evans, the foreman of the erecting shop, accompanying driver H.J. Robinson and his fireman from Swindon Loco. This 'crew' of relatively high-up personnel certainly points towards a serious attempt to try for a high speed.

There is an interesting fact associated with this event, in that inspector Flewellen had been on the footplate of *City of Truro* on the 9th May, 1904 run which resulted in the speed of 102.3 mph being attained briefly down the Whiteball bank. It is said that Churchward had given his blessing to that event (which appears to be the reason why Flewellen was present - inspectors did not usually ride on Ocean Liner specials) to counter the competitive service being run from Plymouth by the LSWR, which was turning in times to Waterloo of just three minutes over four hours. Although, clearly, the Great Western played down the 1904 claim of over 100 mph, maybe the report of this happening left a desire somehow, somewhere, to repeat the performance with a six-coupled engine, more particularly with those who had experienced it. Who better was placed to urge the crew to try it on, but inspector Flewellen, by this time the chief inspector at Swindon.

It was not until 1932 that any account of this run was to appear. The controversy over the *City of Truro* and the 1904 achievement of 102.3 mph still raged. The 'Saint' episode was as a light engine and the method of measuring the speed based on stopwatch observations between mileposts with a cross-check of a rough timing between two signal boxes. This account stems from a communication from Collett in the April 1932 issue of the *Railway Magazine*. Clearly there appears to be some unusual regulator and reverser settings for such a trial without any load, but it is clear that a very high speed was attained. One wonders what the ride would have been like at such a speed, with the two-cylinder layout of this class giving rise to some pretty horrific hammering on the track and springing. Certainly there would have been some uncomfortable moments on the footplate. It has been suggested that the lever reverse, always difficult to move at speed, suddenly shifted into full forward gear when being adjusted, the result being that the engine 'took off'. Bearing in mind that these engines were still unsuperheated, a combination of full regulator and full forward gear would have created a huge demand for steam, threatening to outstrip the injector supply rate. A few traumatic moments probably occurred on the footplate whilst matters were rectified with a wildly surging locomotive threatening to shake itself apart. It is quite understandable that all mention of the episode was suppressed. It was, after all, a rather irresponsible and dangerous exercise. However, it does show that, in his younger days at least, Charles Collett was willing to participate in a risky venture. One thing is certain, Churchward was out of the picture, he would have banned any such trial had he heard of it.

The second standard locomotive to appear was the class '2800' 2-8-0 for heavy freight. Many parts, the boiler, cylinders and valves, much of the motion and connecting rods were common with the 'Saints'. The first of what became a total

The '3100' class 2-6-2T basic design was to be built through to the 1930s in the form of the '3150', '5101', '6100' and '8100' classes. Here No. 3141 of 1906 is pictured in 1914.
R.S. Carpenter Collection

Thirty of the 'County Tank' class 4-4-2Ts were built. No. 2225 of 1905 was captured at Oxford Shed on 21st April, 1934.   *H.F. Wheeller Collection*

A clutch of 'Counties' and Moguls is found at Old Oak Common Shed in the 1920s. Identifiable are Nos. 3803 *County Cork*, 5362 and 4314 with a further 'County' and Mogul in the distance.   *John Scott-Morgan Collection*

of 168 examples appeared in traffic in June 1903. A great workhorse, it was destined to remain in production up to 1942, providing the GWR with a reliable and long-lived freight motive power. Reference 1 in *Table One* refers to this design.

With the express and freight side of things catered for, the next in the standard design list was the class '3100' 2-6-2T for light passenger work over much of the GWR. The drawing office was most certainly busy as the first of these locomotives appeared in September 1903 and entered traffic for trials. By the end of 1908 a further 39 of the '3100' class plus 41 of the slightly more powerful '3150' class were in service.

The final two designs to appear were the 'County' class 4-4-0 in May 1904 and its 'County Tank' 4-4-2T variant in December 1905. Thus, by the end of 1905 five out of the six standard designs were building, so the works were at full stretch as they tooled up for what was to become the most comprehensive standardisation programme in British railway history. Collett's handling, with H.C. King, of this situation certainly ensured that matters ran smoothly to turn out the new locomotive prototypes and production batches as needed. His times of dealing with Churchward and his Chief Assistant, F.G. Wright, were of great benefit for what was to come in his career moves later on. Also his prestige around the works was much enhanced, despite his naturally withdrawn manner, by his polite but firm dealings with the shop foremen.

The 2-6-2T of the '3100' etc. class was restricted from use due to its weight on some of the branch lines, so a lightweight variant, the '4400' class was developed. Only 11 were built, the prototype at Swindon, with the production batch assembled at the small Wolverhampton works of the GWR.

A further 2-6-2T was under development, the '4500' class, but Swindon works was so occupied with all the new builds and general rebuilds that, the production batch of 20 was put out to Wolverhampton. These rather cramped facilities, which needed renewing if construction of locomotives was to continue there, turned out this number in 1906 to 1908. They were, in fact, the last new locomotives to be built there, the works being relegated to a servicing facility only shortly after. There had been a slight reduction in traffic receipts so the GWR Board wished to restrict capital expenditure, Wolverhampton being one of the casualties.

We have also seen the reasoning behind the production of what became an additional standard class, the 'Star' four-cylinder 4-6-0 earlier in this chapter. This was a locomotive to be of great interest to Collett in later years, as it led directly to his 'Castle' and 'King' classes of the 1920s.

Whilst all the above standard locomotives were appearing, there was a major development connected with the ongoing research programme, in that

The '45XX' class 2-6-2T was to be found on much branch work for many years. Here No. 4505 hauls its solitary coach on the Looe branch in the 1950s.   *John Scott-Morgan Collection*

'4300' class 2-6-0 No. 8343 (formerly 5343) arrives at Starcross with a down passenger train from Exeter in the 1930s.   *John Scott-Morgan Collection*

Churchward was serious about continuing this. He obtained funds from the Board to construct a locomotive test plant in 'A' shop. On this an engine could be run on suitably positioned rollers, thus reproducing in a stationary mode what would be found on the road. However, there was an inbuilt disadvantage in this plant in that it could only absorb power outputs of up to 500 horsepower. The large 4-6-0s in production were capable of sustained outputs well in excess of 1,200 horsepower, so any meaningful tests at full power would not be possible except out on the road. It has never been adequately explained why Churchward accepted this major drawback to the testing facilities unique in the railway scene in the UK. He appeared to have lost interest in its potential. It was to remain for Collett to remedy this in later years, as we shall see.

Perhaps Churchward's most reprehensible action occurred in 1906. The old broad gauge 2-2-2 *North Star*, designed and built by R. Stephenson & Co., the first locomotive to haul a passenger train on the GWR, on 31st May, 1838, was cut up for scrap. It had stood preserved in the works since withdrawal in 1871. In addition the only other broad gauge locomotive in existence, the 4-2-2 *Lord of the Isles* was also scrapped. Why Churchward ordered this has never been fully explained, maybe because the former was not a Great Western design he felt that it had little significance in the long line of Swindon products. However, some *North Star* components survived this sabotage, for they are recorded as being used in 1924 when the GWR built a replica for the Stockton & Darlington Centenary Exhibition. This replica lives on in the GWR Museum at Swindon. The *Lord of the Isles* was a classic example of the best of the broad gauge express types, and its loss was a particularly callous example of the lack of appreciation of its historical significance.

As Swindon settled into large scale production, some effort in the drawing office was being ploughed into a radical departure from the normal run of things - a Pacific. The Board had publicity on its mind, publicity involving not only a very large locomotive, but a large locomotive of a wheel arrangement yet to appear in the UK.

Churchward pointed out that this would cut across his standard programme and result in a locomotive with very restricted usage, but was over-ruled by the Board. Starting with the 'Star' class, the drawing office drew up the design, which had a special one-off boiler mounted on extended frames using standard 'Star' cylinders, wheels and motion. There were some inevitable teething troubles, but *The Great Bear*, as it was named, certainly resulted in the achievement of the publicity aim. It was to remain the only Pacific in the UK until the emergence of Gresley's *Great Northern* in 1922.

As Collett prepared for a promotion, for King was moved to the position of Assistant for special duties to Churchward in 1912, two more design exercises were under way, the 2-8-0T for mineral work and the mixed traffic 2-6-0. Only the prototype of the former was constructed in his time as Assistant Works Manager, but series production of the Mogul was under way as 1912 approached. With 11 years of his Assistant's experience behind him, Charles Collett slipped easily into the Works Manager's post in 1912. He was to consolidate his growing prestige at Swindon, and in the war years ahead, to demonstrate his complete mastery of the complexities of production and servicing of the GWR locomotive stock, in addition to the reorganisation of Swindon for munitions' production shortly after hostilities had commenced.

'Star' class No. 4017 *Knight of the Black Eagle*, built in 1908. The location is unknown in this 1910 photograph.   *R.S. Carpenter Collection*

The Great Bear, Churchward's only Pacific at Old Oak Common.   *John Alsop Collection*

Socially, Charles and Ethelwyn kept very much out of the limelight, but clearly had some informal get-togethers with a few of the more senior people. Churchward was certainly one such person who got to know the Colletts outside the works' environment, and his respect for Ethelwyn was demonstrated by asking her to select some names for the 'Star' and 'Saint' classes being built. Now Ethelwyn had considerable Welsh connections and the appearance of some Welsh abbeys in the 'Star' names might well be some of her suggestions. Likewise, her father's clergyman status could well have influenced the selection of a number of the saints in the list for that class.

Churchward was, in 1912, 55 years of age, and could be expected to remain in office for about a further 10 years, and so if the GWR followed its established tradition, Collett could expect to suceed him. Providing, of course, that his performance in this demanding new position was satisfactory. He resolved that this would be the case, as he wished to get back to the design side of things and apply some changes to the rather austere but mechanically sound and reliable Churchward locomotives.

The Assistant Works Manager's post was given to W.A. Stanier, who was to be closely associated with Collett over the following 20 years. Stanier, whose father had been a GWR officer before him, had started as an apprentice in 1892 and was, at an early stage of his career, noticed as having future potential for high office.

One of the first matters to come Collett's way was a general improvement of the works in terms of the equipment employed which involved a substantial investment. It may come as a bit of a surprise that Collett and Stanier were given the opportunity to update the, by now, extensive locomotive works. Churchward, it appears, had been taking advantage of an accounting procedure which should have been curtailed some time before. Railway accounts at that time had a heading 'Maintenance of Locomotives' and any provision in excess of actual expenditure needed to be shown in the accounts as actually spent. When the Chief Accountant prepared the accounts he asked Churchward whether the number of locomotives renewed was adequate, based on their estimated life. The Locomotive Superintendent was prepared to give a theoretical estimate and would agree, say, that 100 were renewed when the actual number was considerably less. This procedure was also applied to the rolling stock and the difference in actual and theoretical expenditure appeared as 'Sundry Outstanding Accounts'. These excess amounts gradually built up over the years and were drawn on as needed for some of the experimental and improvement works in the Superintendent's Department.

Although Churchward was correct in building up a reserve fund, which could help add to the financial stability of the GWR, it was not very good accounting practice to deliberately divert money which could have been used to increase the dividend rate.

When, in later years, Churchward was asked why the General Manager, at that time Sir James Inglis, was not told that the accounts had such reserves hidden away, he replied: 'Had I told him, he would have spent the money!'

By the time all this surfaced, Inglis was dead, Churchward was fast approaching retirement and Grouping was being proposed. The accounting procedures were to be overhauled by the incoming General Manager, Sir Felix Pole and, as Collett took office, the reporting procedures of the GWR were changed such that Pole had much more information at his fingertips, with the chief officers reporting through him to the Board, more in line with procedures on other railways.

G.J. Churchward, a photograph taken about 1918.

STEAM: Museum of the Great Western Railway

Chapter Three

Consolidation and War

Once the '43XX' class 2-6-0 was designed and being built in quantity, Churchward had reached his limit of desired standard types as he himself put it, for some 10 to 15 years, save for perhaps one or two designs for special duty. With the drawing office staff being switched from design and development to other matters, the status quo at Swindon appeared to be set until it was judged necessary to start supplementing the very successful build up of locomotive stock the standardisation programme had produced. It would be a purely production exercise for some time.

With several years as Assistant Works Manager under his belt, Collett began to implement some changes he had quietly planned, now he was in a position to carry them out. One such change was in the boiler shop, where a fitter, F.R. Higgs, was appointed chief boiler foreman, much to the consternation of the boilermakers. However, Collett was proved correct in this appointment, for Higgs was an astute man who concentrated on improving the equipment of the boiler shop which involved, particularly, the heavy flanging and plate forming presses. The undercurrent of feeling regarding this appointment of an 'outsider' smouldered on for many years, until Higgs reached retirement, but Collett's choice was justified by the improved boiler life brought about by the handling of the machinery upgrades introduced. Charles obviously had a clear insight into the choice of a good person capable of overseeing a complex procedure, for such was the GWR boiler manufacture with its special requirements associated with copper fireboxes and the steel Belpaire/tapered boiler structure used on the larger, more important, locomotives.

The reasoning behind the employment of a fitter as boiler shop manager was occasioned by Collett's insistence on improving the precision of boiler manufacture so that a replacement unit fitted the locomotive without the earlier, and sometimes lengthy, matching processes to ensure a good fit. The processing through the works was speeded up, reducing repair costs. This was so effective that in some instances in later years, when Collett was looking for the maximum cost savings, a boiler could be left in place for over 300,000 engine miles - a prodigious figure.

Sometimes Charles' formality led to some amusing incidents on the shop floor. The story is recounted, around this time, of a visit to the boiler shop to inspect a firebox under repair. The shop, at this time, was still lit by gas incandescents, and to inspect the inside of the box, a portable gas flare connected to the mains by a flexible pipe would have been the normal source of illumination. Collett turned to the hovering chargehand and said: 'Fetch me an illuminant'. This request was met with a blank stare. Churchward, who was present, stepped briskly forward and called: 'Bill, bring a bloody gas!'

The Swindon works were a source of pride to Churchward who frequently invited colleagues from the Association of Railway Locomotive Engineers (ARLE) to visit, more especially those who were relatively new members. And

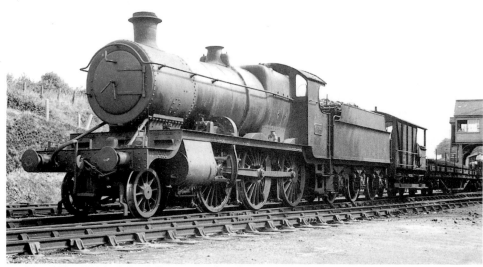

Mogul No. 6354, built by Collett in 1923, has charge of a permanent way train at Perranwell in August 1948.   *R.S. Carpenter/Joe Moss Collection*

One of Collett's improvements to the Churchward 2-6-0 was the introduction of outside steampipes. Here No. 4377, built in 1915 and a Welsh engine all its life, is found at Welshpool on the down 'Cambrian Coast Express' in the 1950s.   *A.V.W. Mace Collection*

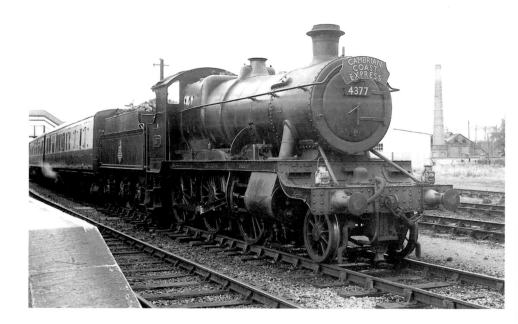

so, in 1913, Charles Collett was told of the imminent arrival of Nigel Gresley, who had been appointed CME of the Great Northern Railway in 1911. He enlisted the help of Stanier to accompany Gresley and himself on a tour of the works. Churchward also came with them but obviously left many of the workshop questions to be parried by Collett and Stanier. Many of the design features of GWR locomotives were explained and Gresley politely listened, noted and gave the general impression of aloofness, much to the concealed annoyance, particularly, of Stanier. Churchward appeared unconcerned at this, he knew full well that Gresley was taking in much that he saw.

Outside of the works, Collett's whole life revolved around Ethelwyn. He clearly was besotted with his quiet, unassuming and faithful wife. An almost protective aura surrounded her, as though excessive contact with those outside their restricted social activities could despoil their closeness. Possibly, the security of a close relationship compensated for his earlier losses of his elder brother and father in those early impressionable years of youth.

Collett and Stanier made a good team in the works, working harmoniously together and building up mutual respect for each other's capabilities. This teamwork was shortly to be needed, as events in Europe were moving relentlessly towards war, which broke out in August 1914. Once it was apparent that there was going to be a long and demanding time for victory to be achieved, the might of the railway works throughout the country was called upon to supplement the inadequate Munitions industry. Henry Fowler, CME of the Midland Railway, was appointed as Director of Production in the Ministry of Munitions and immediately started pressuring the major railway plants throughout the United Kingdom to increase their wartime commitments.

In fact, as soon as the war had broken out, Churchward was eager for the works to be made available for munitions' production. In the context of munitions he saw that anything demanded by the Ministry of Munitions was classified as this. With this liberal interpretation many locomotives and large quantities of stock were supplied throughout the war in addition to the guns, shells and ancilliary equipment more normally classified as such.

Therefore, in keeping with the other railway works in the UK, large parts of Swindon works were turned over to munitions work as 1915 passed, with locomotive building cut back as the wartime obligations absorbed the space. With the requisitioning of numbers of locomotives, mainly Dean Goods 0-6-0s, by the military authorities, the GWR needed replacements to maintain the traffic flow demanded as the country settled into the lengthy war. The 2-6-0 was the best type due to its mixed-traffic capabilities and orders for over 100 were placed throughout the war years, of which 10 were handed over to the Railway Operating Division (ROD) and shipped to France, where they served until 1919.

So far as the immediate effects of the war were concerned, plans had been made prior to the commencement of hostilities for the conversion of existing carriages for an ambulance train. In fact, only 22 days after the declaration of war, the first such train left the works. Some 16 separate trains, involving 238 vehicles, were eventually provided, 12 of which were shipped to the Continent, the remaining four retained for use from the Channel ports.

Dean Goods 0-6-0 No. 2515 at Old Oak Common in 1919.

A fine portrait of Dean Goods No. 2524 on 9th February, 1931   *John Alsop Collection*

Dean Goods No. 2527 at Bristol (St Philip's Marsh) *c.* 1920s.   *R.S. Carpenter Collection*

Such documentation as still exists from World War I days is very sparse and so it is difficult to be exact about the provision of stock built for Government service and wartime use.

The ability of Swindon to cope with the wartime extras in addition to its own commitments to the railway was aggravated by the immediate call-up of workers who were reservists. Something had to give in this drain of skilled hands into the colours - and it was general maintenance that appeared to suffer most. Many apprentices were also permitted to terminate their indentures temporarily to join up. The vast majority of these were guaranteed their jobs back at the end of the war but, of course, many paid the ultimate sacrifice and were never to return. Charles Collett's main task was therefore to ensure that those remaining were deployed in the works, such that the level of manning was sufficient to ensure that the needs of the GWR locomotives and stock, plus the wartime obligations, were adequately covered.

Amongst the first munitions work undertaken at Swindon was an order from the Royal Ordnance Department for fabricated parts for 4.5 inch Howitzers and 60 pounder guns. As these and further orders continued to be placed, Collett was busy reorganising the various shops involved as the output grew to a critical level in 1915. Under pressure from Fowler, a special arrangement was agreed with the War Office, involving the purchase of a considerable amount of machine tools to assist production. In this acquisition, which was adopted, the GWR was permitted to charge their cost to the Government account.

The works became a conglomeration of locomotive and stock production and maintenance intertwined with the output of munitions. One item in production for much of the war was that of cases for 6 inch high-explosive shells, some 2,500 being manufactured each week. The boiler shop had a complete production line for 6 pounder anti-aircraft guns installed, of which some 1,000 were eventually produced. Other minor, but vital, production items were copper driving bands for 18 pounder shells (1,863,000), the reforming of used cartridge cases (5,329,000), and manufacture of graze fuses (343,127) amongst many more ancilliary items as the war progressed. The fuses were put into production following a meeting between Churchward and Henry Fowler, who casually placed a sample on the table and mentioned that this was a typical example produced at the Derby works of the Midland Railway. Upon his return to Swindon Churchward immediately asked Collett and Stanier why could they not do likewise. The challenge was taken up, with the result mentioned above, using part of the cylinder shop.

Locomotive construction continued throughout the war with 175 new engines outshopped. Stock use was very intensive, with no fewer than 37,283 extra passenger trains for military use. The ambulance trains ran some 6,000 journeys and some 550 special leave trains were also provided. The wear and tear on stock and equipment was high indeed, but the excellent mechanical reliability and sturdy construction methods developed at Swindon paid dividends.

Charles Collett's production skills were stretched to the limit and beyond, yet he steadfastly ensured that maximum use of the facilities was made to cope with the demands of those difficult years. Churchward backed him up to the hilt, and recognised in him a worthy successor to himself at retirement. After all in his estimation, the design team was second to none and it really needed a first class production man at the helm to bring the GWR into the post-war era which, he sensed, would not be the same as that existing in pre-war days.

Apart from his general dislike of works' involvement in military work, because of the inevitable disruption this had on the servicing and repairs, Collett most certainly disapproved of Churchward's outdoor pursuits of shooting and fishing, but diplomatically kept these latter thoughts from his chief. Only in later years, when he himself was CME, did he voice opinions as to his dislike of such sporting activities.

The employment of women for some lighter tasks had been mooted, but effectively blocked by Collett on the grounds that the facilities there were geared specifically towards male employment. He could not quite grasp the fact that women were, in many ways, just as capable as men in the lighter realms of the engineering sphere. His upbringing had imbued him with the Victorian middle-class attitude towards the fair sex and its capabilities. In the offices, particularly on the secretarial side, however, Swindon works did employ a growing number of women.

A sensitive person, the feelings Collett had about his chief's pastimes pointed to the fact that he clearly abhorred, not only blood sports, but the war. However, he had sufficient patriotic drive to apply his organisational and management skills to the reorganisation of the works onto a railway and munitions footing. This ensured that the GWR did its bit in boosting the capability of the country to sustain its offensive drive on the Continent. In this, as in the future 1939-45 war, his main concern was for the efficient construction and maintenance of the railway's stock serving the needs of the Country in those difficult years.

One small change which took place in 1916, almost unnoticed in the flurry of war, was that Churchward relinquished the title of Locomotive, Carriage and Wagon Superintendent for that of Chief Mechanical Engineer. This change was in keeping with similar happenings on many of the other railways.

Chapter Four

The Top Job and Grouping

At last the war finished and the railways began to prepare for a change. What that change was to be, at this time, was not yet decided. Nationalisation was in the air, and the ARLE committee which had been drawing up the standard designs for that possibility had prepared a range of locomotives to be considered. This committee had been one on which Churchward had served and which had given him a marvellous forum to propose his design features now so well established on the GWR. Admittedly, Maunsell, on the SE&CR, had adopted the Churchward two-cylinder concept together with the taper boiler and long travel and long lap valves on his prototype 2-6-0 and 2-6-4T, then undergoing trials. But this had been at the instigation of Pearson and Holcroft who had a wealth of experience from their Swindon days, backed up by James Clayton, his chief locomotive draughtsman, following his dealings with Churchward on the ARLE committee. Clayton was an ex-Derby man, who had been seconded to the ARLE committee by Maunsell, who himself was too busy with wartime obligations for the ROD to attend more than a few of the gatherings.

As the railways gathered themselves together after the war, the Swindon works underwent a major expansion, with an anticipated surge in new locomotive building expected. The largest addition was to 'A' shop, which was doubled in size, to almost 11 acres. The 36 100 ft-long pits were increased to 60, and four overhead travelling cranes of 100 tons capacity and 75 ft span installed. Churchward and Collett could foresee a huge increase in demand to come, and started regular discussions as to the way matters might develop in the future.

For his services rendered to the Ministries during the war in connection with the war work carried out at Swindon, Collett was awarded a well-deserved OBE, which was presented to him by the King at an investiture in 1919. Churchward, with a CBE to his credit, was content to sit back and prepare for retirement and promoted Collett from Works Manager to Principal Assistant in 1920. The usual railway habit of letting seniority decide one's successor was a guide to Churchward's choice of Collett as the new CME. William Stanier, who had faithfully served Collett as Assistant Works Manager, was only five years younger, just as capable and, by all accounts, very popular, but had to be content with the Works Manager's post.

The time Collett spent as Assistant to Churchward was profitably spent in building up his expertise on the design side ready for the inevitable rise to CME in a couple of years, for the great man was determined to retire at the end of 1921, when he would be 65. Their deliberations started by revolving around the development of a mixed-traffic version of the 2-8-0 design. This was to become the '4700' class, the prototype of which was fitted, as a temporary measure with the No. 1 boiler whilst the final boiler was being designed. This definitive boiler was to become the No. 7 standard. The remainder of the class, which only totalled nine, was built in 1922-3, as Collett assumed the CME office.

A lightweight task for a '4700' class. A Chester-bound stopping passenger task near Saltney Junction late in the 1930s.   *A.V.W. Mace Collection*

The '4700' class was actually the first to emerge under Collett. Here No. 4703 of the nine-strong class climbs towards Dainton tunnel in the 1940s.   *John Scott-Morgan Collection*

A further deliberation in this 'hand-over' period was an enlarged 'Star', which laid the foundation for Collett's 'Castle' class of 1923. But before any meaningful work on this future project could be instigated, Churchward had authorised a further batch of 12 'Stars' to fill the immediate needs for express work. These, as with the majority of the '4700' class 2-8-0s, were delivered during the first year of Collett's time as CME.

The town of Swindon was closely allied to the GWR works, which had been the catalyst for its emergence on the map. Throughout the years that the town and works had grown together there was always a close relationship. When it acquired Borough status in 1900, following the merger of Old Swindon with New Swindon, and local officials were elected, it was Churchward, as a much respected resident in high office with the GWR, who was elected as the first Mayor. This selection of eminent railway personnel continued in 1921, when Charles Collett was offered, and accepted, the status of a Justice of the Peace for the Swindon bench. Maybe Churchward had had a hand in this local honour, in that it would propel Collett into the community and make him better known amongst the populace. (Although, not having had shop-floor experience made him a shadowy, remote, figure even to many of the workforce.) The authoritarian stance of Churchward, coupled with a down-to-earth manner, had earned that CME much respect amongst the workers. With Collett remaining very much to himself and keeping all but his immediate assistants at a distance, a change in attitude gradually assumed itself; this was mollified considerably by the presence of Stanier who to all intents and purposes was the CME in the context of actual shop-floor interchanges. Collett only appeared down there when absolutely required. At least he did realise this and was happy to let his deputy deal with many works problems - and much else outside of the works in the local community. Whether, for external matters, it was just plain disinterest in things outside of his expertise, or just a hint of snobbishness, is a matter of debate.

Grouping was on the cards, following the Railways Act of 1921, but the GWR standardisation programme was now so well entrenched and, with the certain knowledge that the railway would not be materially altered, other than a moderate expansion in the Welsh area, this ensured that Swindon would remain as the prime supplier of motive power. Those small railways absorbed by the GWR that had their own works were, for the most part, only geared for heavy maintenance, not construction. Thus Swindon designs were to be continued along the development path laid down over the latter years of Churchward's incumbency.

A measure as to how the railway's income was eroded by the effects of World War I can be gauged by the wages bill. In 1913 wages took 40 per cent of income, in 1923 this had risen to 60 per cent. With shareholders taking a further 10 per cent in dividends, there was not much left over to finance the upkeep of buildings, communications, locomotives, rolling stock and track at a time when they were all very run down. The maximum contribution which had been wrung out of the Government for the GWR was a mere £15 million. It is against a background of tight expenditure levels that Collett began as CME.

Upon taking office, on 1st January 1922, Collett began to think about a Principal Assistant, but bided his time, before deciding that Stanier would be most appropriate for the post. He and Stanier had worked together for over 10

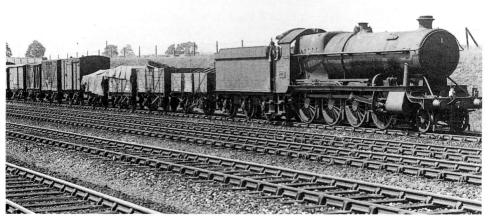

This depiction of '4700' class No. 4704 on a more mundane freight task was taken in the 1940s near Reading.   *John Scott-Morgan Collection*

A down cattle train passing Swindon, a last duty in 1955 for 'Star' class No. 4062 *Malmesbury Abbey*, one of the batch ordered by Collett shortly after he became CME. Note the external steam pipes of this batch.   *R.S. Carpenter Collection*

years and had struck up a harmonious working relationship. The important feature of trust in both parties was there and the future developments of GWR motive power were to show their respective hands as a competent design and production partnership. It was not until 1923 that Stanier received his promotion to Principal Assistant after three years as Works Manager. He was ultimately to be given most of the tasks external to the works involving local affairs, Charles Collett's retiring personality never encouraging him to get too involved in such matters. Stanier's affable, outgoing, personality was eminently suited to these jobs delegated to him.

As had Churchward before him, Collett initially reported directly to the Board through the Locomotive Committee of the Directors and also attended Board meetings. However, Felix Pole, the new General Manager had other plans for the CME's department. In 1923 he ordered that, henceforth, the CME should report through himself as was already normal on the other railways.

Much more capable of dealing with works problems than Churchward had been, the new working hours regulations and the greater power of Trades Unions brought Collett more into contact with shop floor representatives. Polite and firm with them, he gained from them a degree of respect and caution when dealing with their demands. He could, of course, deflect some of the requests from Unions to Pole who, as General Manager, had more say as to the outcome of their demands.

The first noticeable change on the GWR came about shortly after Collett assumed his new responsibility, and this was the reintroduction of the old GW livery of chocolate and cream for carriage stock, Churchward having dispensed with this in preference for a deep red in 1908. The opportunity to make this change was brought about by the need to attend to the general run-down state of much of the carriage stock, caused by the lack of maintenance and repainting during the war.

One little matter which came to his notice shortly after taking office was that of the Vale of Rheidol narrow gauge locomotives, for in 1922 the GWR had absorbed the Cambrian Railways which included this small line. Two new 2-6-2 tanks were specified and the order placed on Swindon. Apparently, the GWR Board expected two new engines to be delivered in the early summer of 1922. The drawing office was, in fact, busy on so many other items that the narrow gauge engines were on a very low priority, as Collett mentioned in a very testy letter to the Chairman after receiving a rather critical memorandum asking why Swindon was not following this up urgently. The Chairman got the point and withdrew the demands. At least this episode showed Charles Collett leaping to the defence of his hard-pressed staff.

The two locomotives in question were eventually designed and constructed. Due to their narrow gauge format little in the way of standard parts could be employed save some boiler mountings and cylinders, the latter taken from the railmotor vehicles.

The position of CME carried with it certain external responsibilities, one of which concerned the Park in Swindon. Since the early days of the GWR presence in Swindon, the recreation of the inhabitants was provided for in part by a cricket ground located south of St Mark's Church. The land for this had been presented by a Colonel Vilett. The earliest record of matches being played on this ground dates from 1854.

Vale of Rheidol narrow gauge 2-6-2T No. 7, one of the pair built at Swindon in 1924 under Collett, is seen when nearly new at Aberystwyth VoR station.   *R.S. Carpenter Collection*

The Park, Swindon as it is to be found today. St Mark's church, built by the GWR for its employees, is to be seen through the trees in the distance.   *Author*

Later, in about 1873, this ground became known as the GWR Park and it was run by a committee drawn from the top management of the works. The chairman of this committee was invariably the Locomotive Superintendent. The cricket was eventually moved to another ground and the Park became exclusively used for other recreational pursuits. One such event was the annual Children's Fete organised by the Mechanics Institute. This became a big social event for the town, and by 1904 was attracting some 38,000 attendees.

When Charles Collett became CME, he found that there was a marked fall-off in the use of the facility. On 6th February 1922, the Park committee was convened under Collett and the possibility of the GWR relinquishing the responsibility for the Park discussed. Matters were aired with the Swindon Borough Council and, on 30th June, 1925, the GWR Park was handed over to that authority, the GWR receiving in exchange a parcel of land to the north of the carriage and wagon works needed for expansion of that facility. Although he was never keen on involvement in external affairs, Charles Collett nevertheless made sure that the GWR did not lose out in this negotiation.

With the departure of Churchward, the drawing office staff noticed a distinct withdrawal of personal collaboration from the CME's office, although Stanier still made his presence felt. The days were gone when Churchward would come out into the office, perch himself on one of the stools, and gather staff around him for a friendly and helpful discussion. Charles Collett sat aloof in his office, not often to make contact with the draughtsmen, and took under his wing all major decisions. When it came to technical reports or analysis, those responsible for these were rarely seen and, even more rarely, given commendations. It was as though he found it difficult to place absolute trust upon their work, save for a very select few.

Charles and Ethelwyn had, in November 1921, celebrated their silver wedding anniversary and were looking forward to many more happy years together. There were no children, but the stability of steady married life had been of great help in those busy wartime days. Much as they tried, the staff in the design office could never get Charles to enter into any of their social functions. He remained very much to himself outside the work environment, and had always found it difficult to mix with others outside the office. Ethelwyn was the centre of his life away from work, and they were rarely seen at any of the Swindon events. Their only known pastime outside of the home was a weekly trip to the cinema, usually on a Tuesday evening. However, Charles' J.P. status did involve him to some degree in the business of the borough and Ethelwyn quietly supported him by involving herself in various town bodies.

As Churchward continued to live at Newburn House, originally built for Joseph Armstrong when he became Locomotive Superintendent in 1864 and known locally as Churchward's House, Charles and Ethelwyn could not take up residence there. But they were quite happy to stay in No. 5, Church Place, after all, it was most conveniently close to the works entrance.

However, despite Collett being a difficult person to work with, he was recognised as a competent engineer and skilled organiser by the staff. His engineering perception was firmly grounded in Churchward's practices and contained here, perhaps, was one negative feature, which permeated through all developments and

2-8-0 No. 2866, built 1919, has a long train of up coal empties in hand in the Brent-Dainton ares, seen in the early 1950s. *John Scott-Morgan Collection*

No. 5, Church Place, to be the home of Collett whilst CME. *Author*

new designs, during his term as CME. The particular item in question was that of superheating, the GWR philosophy as laid down by Churchward being to adopt a moderate degree of superheating. With the excellent steaming boilers of 225 psi and the free-running characteristics of long lap, long travel valves, the premier GWR engines were not in need of high degree superheating, provided the fuel quality remained high. However, an adoption of high degree superheating would most certainly have turned excellent locomotives into outstanding examples of steam power, yet Collett clung tenaciously to the Churchward principle.

One positive attitude which Collett did display was that of being willing to enter into some dialogue with Trades Union representatives from the works. Churchward and, indeed during his time as CME, the GWR as a company, never recognised Trades Unions. It took the 1914 Government take-over for the war to make unions recognised, once implemented an irreversible decision. Therefore, after the railways returned to their pre-war management style this was part of the status quo to be absorbed by Management. This single change appeared to be one of the major deciding factors which persuaded Churchward that it was time to go. His enshrined autocratic ways were not compatible with this major shift in industrial relations. Management styles had changed dramatically in the first two decades of the century and Collett had advanced with them, his younger age making him more amenable and understanding in connection with such developments. A more open relationship between Management and workers was beneficial to the smooth running of the works, he reasoned.

A further fact was that Churchward, being a bachelor, had not been tempered by family life and his approach to personal matters was, on occasions, somewhat harsh and undiplomatic. Collett, however, had a very close relationship with his wife and this clearly affected his handling of sensitive issues to some considerable degree.

One further feature of Collett's time as CME was that he did not approve of his staff paying visits to other railway works. To him the GWR was thought to be streets ahead of all others and needed no input of 'foreign' ideas. Perhaps had such visits been encouraged and the employment of high-degree superheating been noted, a change in policy at Swindon might have occurred earlier. It is of note that, just about 10 years later, after his move to the LMS as CME, Stanier quickly realised the benefits of going to high-degree superheating and changed his ways. He was flexible enough to realise that some Swindon ideas were not always the best, and that progress was being ignored in the interests of standardisation not only of parts, but in design philosophy.

The rather inward-looking policy of Collett, although disheartening for those beneath him, was at least tempered with a sound engineering perception such that his locomotive developments were almost entirely successful. But, of course, Churchward had laid such a forward-looking standardisation policy, all Collett really needed to do was to continue the cycle of improvements on sound designs which had been discussed before he (Churchward) had retired. However, having said all this there were some episodes which led to his worth being impressed on the team he inherited. Perhaps the following example is a particularly good illustration.

One of the important matters brought to his attention on his taking office was a request from the GWR Board for the locomotive works to reduce expenditure by half a million pounds per year, a considerable sum in those days (equivalent to £25 million today). As an immediate measure, several hundred workers were laid off, but further economies were clearly needed to reach the savings target. Some measure of cost reduction could be had by examining engines more thoroughly as they approached intermediate or general repair. Collett, using his considerable works' experience, ordered that if boilers were still in relatively good condition the amount of remedial work on them must be restricted to that needed for a return to service, rather than an exchange of the unit. Also, he instigated studies to see how mileages between repairs could be extended.

The increased mileages obtained between shopping eventually reduced the maintenance bills and contributed towards bringing the works' costs down to a more acceptable level. After this, he was always looking for ways to keep maintenance costs to an acceptable level. Future technical advances were scrutinised and, if potential was evident, implemented such that Swindon works' efficiency was amongst the best in the Country.

A small, but significant, cost-saving measure exercised at Charles' start as CME was the order that bogie brakes, a Churchward fad, were no longer to be included on any new locomotives. He also stipulated that those engines already fitted should have them removed during overhaul. No one had dared suggest this in Churchward's days, the 'Old Man' would not have approved.

One administrative change made by Collett shortly after becoming CME was to change the title of the Outdoor Assistant to that of Locomotive Running Superintendent and Outdoor Assistant to the CME. The cessation of the old system of one driver/one engine meant that the rostering of footplate staff became all-important if maximum efficiency was to be achieved following the recently introduced eight hour working day. In the earlier days the CME had been in control of drivers and firemen in addition to the locomotives. The new appointment split the responsibility of the holder to the Running Superintendent for running matters and the CME for day to day maintenance and shopping for heavy repairs. The first such holder of this new position was Charles Crump, who had started his career at the GWR works in Wolverhampton, where he rose on the engineering side to become chief draughtsman, before being transferred to Swindon when the design offices at Wolverhampton were closed down.

Further management changes were being proposed by Felix Pole, the new General Manager. Pole wished to change the upper management structure to American lines whereby all departments were to be co-ordinated under one head (a President) for daily operational and financial matters, while an upper strata of top management (vice-Presidents) took decisions on expenditure and policy. Collett recognised in Pole's proposal that the autonomy of the Locomotive Department would be broken and accordingly resisted this major change, as it would take financial matters out of his hands. Also its implementation would have brought the running matters under the control of the Superintendent of the Line. He therefore issued a Minute, barely a week after taking control as CME, whereby he ordered that the Divisional boundaries should 'as and when the opportunity offered' be synchronised. This effectively blocked Pole's proposal to split the locomotive and traffic aspects into two separate areas. The GWR mangement structure was to remain essentially the same for most of his time as CME.

Chapter Five

The 'Castle' Beginnings and Personal Tragedy

At the January 1922 meeting of the ARLE, Charles Collett's election to membership was approved, whilst Churchward, as he was now retired, was made an Honorary Member.

Collett was one of the 23 who attended this meeting and who took an active part in the discussions on technical matters. The items listed for this gathering were the standardisation of rivets, the area of opening for safety valves and the measurement of coal consumption of individual engines. On the matter of safety valves, Sir Vincent Raven argued for the Ross pop type but Collett mentioned the fact that the GWR had tried it, but found no material advantage, and they intended to stay with their present type. GWR enginemen much preferred to run with a 'feather' of steam issuing rather than the explosive heavy loss of steam associated with the Ross type.

As Charles began his 19½ years as CME, Churchward was remembered by the workforce in the form of a collection made in his honour in which over £500 was subscribed. He was persuaded to take the gift of a fishing rod bought out of this considerable sum, equivalent to £25,000 today. The residue, which was a tidy sum, he ordered placed into a fund which gave awards to engineering apprentices for good academical work at local technical colleges. This became known as the Churchward Testimonial Fund. The presentation of this took place at the Mechanics Institute at Swindon in April 1922 with the large hall packed to capacity with staff and workers from every department of the GWR. Collett could not be present, being away in Europe on business.

One of Churchward's last proposals for a new express locomotive, which he clearly saw as being needed to cope with the increase in traffic once the war was over and the country settled back to normality, was for developments of both the the 'Stars' and 'Saints'. These designs would have used a larger No. 7 boiler and resulted in weights beyond those which the Civil Engineer was prepared to tolerate over the lines in, particularly, the West Country. As the 'Stars' and 'Saints' were already at the point where a weight increase would compromise the route availability, the proposals died.

The transition to Collett stamping his own authority on the designs to emerge was evident when the first locomotive to be attributed to him appeared, the 'Castle' class. The development of this, to become something of a milestone in the continual search for technical advances in the UK, is chronicled in this Chapter. As we shall see, features of this new express class were to be reflected in British locomotive designs elsewhere over the rest of the decade, and had a profound effect on attitudes towards coal consumption levels.

As Collett consolidated himself into the CME's position, he immediately began to see what could be done to satisfy the by now urgent need for more powerful locomotives. The result was a compromise which resulted in the greatest increase in boiler size compatible with retaining the current route availability. Bearing in mind the Ivatt dictum that the capacity of a boiler/firebox to boil water was the keystone of any locomotive, in other words, the steaming ability, he designed a boiler which was larger than the No. 1 as used on the 'Stars' and 'Saints', but significantly lighter than the No. 7 proposed earlier. The steaming increase was obtained by adding one foot to the length of the firebox, giving an additional 12 per cent in grate area. This resulted in a similar increase to the length of the rear of the frames, which had the bonus of him being able to provide a more spacious cab. To utilise the greater steaming capacity of the boiler, the cylinder diameter was increased to 16 inches, this being possible by reducing tyre size and clearances on the bogie. The motion and chassis were substantially as for the earlier locomotives, so much detail design was common, and tooling was kept to a minimum. In fact the early drawing for the cylinders was merely the 'Star' drawing amended in red to indicate the relevant dimensions which had changed.

With this design, Collett produced the styling which was to remain with all GWR tender locomotives built at Swindon to the end of steam. The 'Castle' class, as these were to be known, was to be a turning point in locomotive development which had a profound effect upon other railways, such was their capability and economy in service. An initial batch of 10 of what was to become a classic locomotive was ordered in 1922.

As the prototype 'Castle' was being schemed in the drawing office, Grouping was approaching and the ARLE members were busy at the 23rd October, 1922 meeting in discussing the impact this would have on their membership, as the number of independent locomotive engineers of their kind would be drastically reduced. Sir Vincent Raven voiced the opinion that it might well be necessary to have senior and junior groups. Collett stated his views, these unfortunately not being minuted, and, after the meeting, returned to Swindon to reflect on this matter.

In his usual desire to keep abreast of new technology and developments, Charles Collett noted with interest that Sir Vincent Raven was due to speak to the GWR (London) Lecture and Debating Society at Paddington on 4th January, 1923. He announced his intention of being present and was offered the chair for that meeting, and took that offer up. The subject to be covered at this event was 'Railway Electrification'. In fact, as far back as 1892, William Dean had been asked by the then GWR Chairman to make enquiries of R.W. Crompton, one of the leading electrical engineers of the day, of the possibility of using electric locomotives for the Severn Tunnel railway. However, little appears to have been done following an initial meeting between Dean and Crompton and the proposal died. Electricity was then still a relatively new science and not treated with sufficient enthusiasm by many of the older school of engineers in the closing years of the 19th century.

Sir Vincent was, at the time of Grouping, tipped to be offered the post of CME of the newly-formed London and North Eastern Railway (LNER) and, clearly, was interested in promoting the North Eastern Railway's (NER) plans to electrify the York to Newcastle main line which were still on the table. He had, recently, designed and constructed a huge 4-6-4 electric express locomotive, but this awaited the main line upgrade which never happened. The two electrification schemes which the NER had successfully applied were the Newcastle suburban and the Newport-Shildon freight services. Both were technically successful and Raven, in his paper, drew heavily on the results obtained by these applications of electric traction.

Collett, at the end of Raven's talk, opened the discussion by stating that what they had heard had given all present a great deal to think over. Electric traction certainly had distinct advantages over steam locomotives, which themselves could be viewed as a power-house on wheels. After posing the question: why do we not drive our railways by electric traction, Collett then raised the issue of the cost of doing so. This cost was in providing the power stations and sub-stations to feed the current to the railway. (It should be noted that in the years considered here there was no National Grid system for providing economic electricity throughout the Country, this was to be initiated later in 1923 by the Central Electricity Generating Board, but was not to be completed until 1933.) Having earlier mentioned the Swiss application of electric power to their railways being occasioned by the lack of affordable coal, he then suggested that electric power sources could be provided by building power stations in coalfield areas, citing South Wales as an example. Many of the early railway electrification schemes incorporated a dedicated power station to produce the current required, so Collett was perfectly justified in pressing home the point of power supply as being a major investment. On this rather tenuous argument he then asked for comments from the floor.

The GWR Electrical Engineer, R.T. Smith, who was present, stated that despite some 900 miles of track electrified throughout the UK, these were mainly suburban in nature, whereas Sir Vincent had specifically covered main line applications. He agreed that, with power sources available locally, South Wales could make a good case for electric traction, the traffic being very similar to the Newport-Shildon line of the NER. The cost of electric locomotives was some 50 per cent greater than an equivalent steam locomotive, but this had to be balanced against the fact that one electric locomotive could do the work of two steam locomotives. The major capital cost was therefore the cost of obtaining an electricity supply and the modifications needed to adapt the track.

Electrification on the GWR never really got taken seriously, with Collett always worried about the cost of obtaining supplies and the Civil Engineers concerned about the cost of modifying and then maintaining the track and equipment. Steam was set to continue as motive power. Future studies on electrification were carried out, as will be mentioned in Chapter Twelve, but the reason for these was for other purposes associated with coal supplies.

The first ARLE meeting to be held after Grouping took place on the 19th January, 1923. Raven was there as President still, as the LNER CME had yet to be chosen, but the impact of the reorganisation of the railways was apparent in those attending:

C.B. Collett (CME GWR)	George Hughes (CME LMS)
Sir Henry Fowler (Deputy CME LMS)	R.E.L. Maunsell (CME SR)
G.T. Glover (CME GN of Ireland)	R.L. Reid (C&W Superintendent LMS)
A.J. Hill (Late CME GER)	G.H. Wild (CME Dublin & SE, Ireland)

The main topic of discussion was, obviously, membership, with George Hughes suggesting a very wide membership. Charles Collett countered this by stating that if Hughes' suggestion was to be taken literally, some 53 of his staff would be eligible to attend meetings. Gresley, not present for this meeting, had sent a letter in which he stated that the individual CME should have the final decision on which of his staff were to attend. Obviously, opinions differed somewhat amongst those participating and so a committee was appointed to review the rules of ARLE membership. This group consisted of Collett, Glover, Gresley, Hill, Hughes and Maunsell, with Fowler as Secretary.

This committee met in early February and swiftly drew up the new rules which basically meant that CMEs and their deputies plus C&W Superintendents should be eligible. Members should not exceed six for any railway in Great Britain. The CMEs of the four main Irish Railways were also to be eligible. Although there is no record to be found of the formal adoption of these rules, this appears to be the broad outline of future membership of the ARLE.

The second complete year of Collett's tenure as CME, 1923, started with, for him, a huge personal tragedy. Quite suddenly, after a short time of illness, Ethelwyn died. The illness was sudden and catastrophic, being acute nephritis (kidney failure) coupled with pleurisy. Once diagnosed, full time nursing care was called for and a distraught Charles sent for Ethelwyn's cousin, Enid Thomas, to come and be at her side. Enid lived in Caerphilly and speedily journeyed to Swindon. The doctor's prognosis was not at all good, nephritis could be fatal, and Charles was overcome with grief at the thought of losing his wife, to whom he was so attached. The end came finally on 18th March, 1923 at home, No. 5, Church Place. She was only 47, and Charles was devastated at his loss, Ethelwyn had been the core of his life outside the works. His staff noticed an immediate change in their leader in that his already very private life became even more private. Work was the only subject permitted when in his presence, all external meetings were boycotted and, even more worrying for those under him, there was a marked change in Charles' health. Weight seemed to slip off him and his tall figure grew thin and wasted. It was as though his hold on life was slipping away, Ethelwyn had meant so much to him.

Stanier found himself, at the start of his Assistant's job, delegated to take on most of Collett's outside responsibilities as the distraught CME retreated into himself. However, the well-knit team in the design offices pulled together and continued their tasks without any slackening of purpose under the watchful guidance of Stanier.

Although the very centre of Charles' home life had fallen apart, there was still much to keep his mind occupied in working hours. There was a lot to be dealt with in the drive to bring out the new 4-6-0 on schedule, in addition to dealing with the 900 plus extra locomotives acquired from the minor Welsh railways absorbed at Grouping. The need to attend all this gradually took hold and overcame his domestic sorrows. He once again began to grasp the reins of power more securely.

In choosing his successor, Churchward had most certainly realised that in Collett he had someone capable of continuing his programme of locomotive developments. After all, as far as he was concerned it would be mainly a production exercise, and this was a sphere in which Collett excelled. There was also the fact that Stanier was some five years Collett's junior and the habit of letting seniority reign caused selection of the latter. The negativity which this eventually implied took some years to show through, for Churchward's designs were years ahead of many of those on the other railways and fully capable of carrying out most of the tasks expected of them. The design changes to cater for heavier loads would be minimal.

The fact that for almost 20 years Collett had been involved in the running of the production matters in the locomotive works, and had limited say in the design sphere, meant that his design experience was grounded in the last days of Dean's incumbency. He had not been involved in the all-important design exercises leading to the successful range of locomotives in service by the time Churchward retired. It was only natural that he kept closely to the Churchward precepts and the effects of the sudden loss of his wife may have stifled any desire to launch out with a completely new design of express locomotive, particularly after the affair of the 0-6-2T, described fully in Chapter Eight.

Nowadays, after a bereavement such as Charles Collett had experienced, there are many types of support for those grieving. Having no immediate family, Collett would have had little close support at a critical time. He would have been left largely alone. Those at work were never close to him and rarely taken into his confidence apart from, perhaps, Stanier. He had only been CME for a little over a year and quite probably still felt vulnerable as he continued to establish his mode of control.

It was shortly after his recovery that he was returning from a meeting at Paddington one evening with one of his junior works officials, K.J. Cook. Their conversation eventually turned to a problem concerning several recent failures of 'Stars' caused by the fracturing of connecting rod small ends. These failures had resulted in major damage to the cylinders involved, when the pistons, now free of the small end, slammed through the front covers. All the engines concerned were on Plymouth to Paddington expresses and had run about 200 miles of this journey when the failure occurred. Collett was obviously very concerned about these failures and asked Cook to find as many samples of small end bushes as were in the works from 'Stars' under overhaul.

The next morning, he convened a meeting in his office, with Hannington, the Works Manager, Gooderson the 'A' machine shop foreman, Stanier and Cook. The latter had managed to locate several examples which showed signs of damage, and these, together with the parts of the broken rods pointed to lubrication shortage causing seizure and subsequent failure of the bearing, which transmitted the piston pull or thrust to the connecting rod.

The oil reservoir which lubricated the small end was redesigned on Collett's orders from its original rather small size, to a much larger oilbox lying on top of the connecting rod, which used the reciprocating motion to throw the oil to the supply valve at the top of the bearing bush. All existing locomotives were so modified and the future production series all used this new lubrication method, which cured the problem effectively.

The first batch of 'Castles' appeared between August 1923 and April 1924. Collett was certainly proud of his new creation, particularly as it had been dubbed the 'most powerful passenger train engine in the Kingdom'. Breaking away from the then current tradition of keeping details of locomotive performance very much within the bounds of the GWR, he prepared a paper to be given at the First World

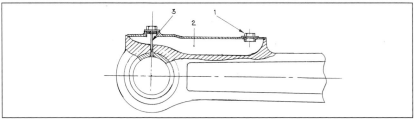

The little end lubrication answer. The filling plug (1) enables the reservoir (2) on the connecting rod to be filled. The reciprocating action throws the oil onto the needle (3) and a flat on this feeds the oil to the bearing.

An early view of Collett 'Castle' class 4-6-0 No. 4073 *Caerphilly Castle* at rest at Old Oak Common. *John Alsop Collection*

No. 5000 *Launceston Castle* stands outside Bristol Old Station signal box. In this view the tender carries the GWR roundel logo. *John Alsop Collection*

Power Conference in London in 1924. This was entitled 'Testing of Locomotives on the Great Western Railway', and included some startling data on coal consumption which made the other British locomotive engineers sit up with what amounted to disbelief. At that time, it was thought that coal consumption per drawbar horsepower hour of 4 lb. was excellent, with most other railways' locomotives returning values of between 4 to 6 lb. Collett's claim was for a staggering 2.83 lb. The significance of the GWR coal consumption claim could be interpreted as a 7½ per cent improvement of that already obtainable from the 'Star' class 4-6-0, according to examination of a figure shown in Collett's paper comparing the two classes on a coal per mile basis. Swindon had, up to now, kept any details of the Churchward design well under wraps. So the revelation that, for some years now, with the 'Star' a figure of a little over 3.0 to 3.25 lb. per drawbar horsepower had been the norm, was to galvanise some of the CMEs into action. In addition, the initial shock of this revelation was compounded by the 'most powerful' claim, particularly when *Caerphilly Castle* was exhibited alongside the LNER *Flying Scotsman* at the Empire Exhibition at Wembley in 1924. The disparity in size between the two locomotives most certainly put this claim to a test. The result was the famous locomotive exchange between the GWR and LNER of 1925 which once and for all proved the superiority of the smaller GWR engine.

The net result of these trials was that Gresley immediately saw the benefits of long lap, long travel valves, and made plans to alter his Pacific design to incorporate this feature. It is notable that Maunsell on the Southern had already adopted such valve events as far back as 1917 on his prototype 2-6-0, but then, he had the expertise of Holcroft and Pearson, both great champions of Churchward and the GWR, to advise him on this, coupled with Clayton's dealings with Churchward on the ARLE standard locomotive design committee during the latter years of the war.

Touching on the naming of express engines, when Collett was busy on the design of the 'Castle' class, the question of names must have been broached. By the time the selection had to be made, Ethelwyn was dead and could no longer be asked for suggestions. However, it is noticeable that out of the first batch of 10, no fewer than five bore the names of Welsh castles. The first example, No. 4073, was *Caerphilly Castle*, the home town of several of his late wife's relations. One likes to think that Ethelwyn would have approved of this gesture.

The 11th 'Castle' to appear from Swindon Works was not a new locomotive, but a rebuild, having been concocted from *The Great Bear* when it became due for a major overhaul. It has often been hinted that Charles Collett had the only Pacific to be built by the GWR destroyed because he was somewhat jealous of Churchward's reputation in connection with it. In fact, the more correct story is rather different - in late 1923, the locomotive was due a new boiler and firebox. Being a 'one-off', there was no spare and a replacement would have to be provided. Boilers, especially non-standard ones, are an expensive item and the cost of providing the replacement ruled out any economic overhaul. *The Great Bear*, due to its weight, was restricted to the main line between London and Bristol and could not be usefully employed on any of the major West Country expresses, unless an engine change was made at Bristol, though there are references to a few visits to Newton Abbot and Wolverhampton. Collett discussed matters briefly with Stanier and then took it upon himself to order the withdrawal of the engine

In 1934, a batch of 10 'Castles' was ordered, to become Nos. 5023-5032. Here No. 5026 *Criccieth Castle* is partially completed.   *R.S. Carpenter Collection*

'Castle' class 4-6-0 No. 4016 *The Somerset Light Infantry*, originally named *Knight of the Golden Fleece* leaves Newton Abbot on an up express *c.*1947-48.   *John Scott-Morgan Collection*

Between 1937 and 1940 a batch of 10 'Stars' was withdrawn and rebuilt as 'Castles'. This view depicts No. 5090, formerly No. 4070, at Stafford Road Shed in 1961. It still retains its old name, *Neath Abbey*. *R.S. Carpenter Collection*

The quality of the coal seems dubious as No. 5021 *Whittington Castle* takes water at Truro, August 1948. *R.S. Carpenter/Joe Moss Collection*

One of the many 'Castles' named after Welsh castles, No. 5026 *Criccieth Castle*, by the 1950s has been modified with a double chimney, here seen at Stafford Road Shed with plenty of steam to spare.   *R.S. Carpenter Collection*

One of the 'Castles' to receive the names from the 'Dukedog' rebuilds, No. 5043 *Earl of Mount Edgcumbe*, formerly *Barbury Castle*, at Shrewsbury in 1960. Yet another example to receive a double chimney.   *R.S. Carpenter Collection*

and its rebuilding as a 'Castle'. The wheels, motion, frames and tender were retained for the rebuild, which emerged from Swindon Works in 1924 and subsequently was named *Viscount Churchill* after the GWR Chairman.

When it was realised by some Board members that the prestige engine was being scrapped, some testy questions were asked of Collett to explain his actions. The GWR had for years been using the status this locomotive gave the railway and it frequently appeared in the publicity issued. Charles turned on his considerable engineering expertise and eventually placated the ruffled Board members, making a strong case for the rebuild on economic grounds. Matters died down and relations between Swindon and Paddington returned to normal.

The policy of naming engines, on the GWR, was extended by Collett to cover not only the main express classes, but eventually to the mixed-traffic classes as well. The names chosen were usually approved via the CME's office. CBC (as he was known amongst the senior staff) could remember the names associated with specific engine numbers, and kept records in his office of all such combinations, including any name change carried out during the life of a locomotive. His memory for detail was nothing short of phenomenal, a feature which clearly helped in his grasp of Swindon works matters through the years.

At the beginning of 1924, the GWR Board announced that a Royal visit to Swindon Works was imminent. King George V and Queen Mary were to come down to Swindon on the GWR Royal Train to make the first official Royal visit to the town, culminating in a tour of the GWR works. So, on the 28th April, Charles Collett received the King and Queen at the Sheppard Street entrance of the carriage works. He presented Stanier and the Carriage Works Manager, F.T.J. Evans, to the Royal visitors. The tour commenced in the immaculately tidied carriage works showing the visitors the various stages in carriage manufacture.

Following this, accompanied by Collett, Stanier, the GWR Chairman, Viscount Churchill, and the General Manager, Felix Pole, they then crossed to the other side of the main line to visit the locomotive works, commencing in the foundry. The Royal visitors were then taken to watch a '4300' class 2-6-0 running at high speed on the stationary test plant. Following this, 'A' shop was toured to demonstrate the manufacturing techniques involved in locomotive construction. One of the 100 ton travelling cranes was put to use to move a completed locomotive, an impressive demonstration.

By now the Royal Train had been brought from Swindon station and parked in a siding alongside the works. Coupled to it was a recently completed 'Castle' class, No. 4082 *Windsor Castle*, for the return journey to London. A temporary platform had been erected there, and the King and Queen were invited onto the locomotive footplate by Sir Felix Pole, who asked the King if he would care to drive the engine a short distance. His Majesty was clearly excited at this possibility and listened carefully to driver Rowe and fireman Cook as they briefly explained the function of the main controls. Queen Mary stood smiling encouragement and carefully holding on to the cab pillar with a piece of white cloth to protect her gloves. The King waited for the Guard to give the 'right away' and then opened the regulator slowly. The Royal Train steamed gracefully away from the works, to the cheers of the workforce who lined the track, until Swindon station was reached, where the King somewhat reluctantly climbed down to board the train for the remainder of the journey back to London.

Chapter Six

Mixed Traffic and the 'Halls'

Before launching into the mixed-traffic developments, a short aside covering the switch from internal to external supply of electricity to Swindon Works is relevant. Gas was still a major source of energy for generating electrical power in the works and in July 1923 a Mr J.A. Robinson, Consulting Engineer to the Metropolitan Vickers Electrical Company, was commissioned to advise on the current power sourcing. The following March his report arrived, recommending the construction of a central steam-powered generating station to replace the numerous gas powered stations then in use. However, the gasworks had just been extended at some expense and Collett was not in favour of the £105,000 cost of Robinson's proposal, arguing that a further three gas engine generating sets would suffice to meet the demand estimated. His arguments were made forcefully enough to get the Board's approval for this rather than the outside recommendation.

However, events in the town were to alter Collett's plans. The demand for more electrical power was being felt in Swindon and the Borough Corporation was preparing for extensions to the generating capacity available. The original power station, in the centre of the town, was to be replaced by a larger plant. An offer was made to the GWR to provide sufficient capacity in this new plant to cater for the needs of both the works and the town. Collett was pleased to accept this as it enabled him to argue against the pressure still on him to provide the steam-operated plant as recommended by Robinson. An agreement with the Corporation was reached and the building of the new power station, sited at Moredon, was started with power supply commencing in 1926.

Strangely, with the introduction of the new electric plant, little was done in respect of the works lighting, this remaining gas until the blackout precautions instituted in World War II demanded good lighting at all hours. Only then was adequate electric lighting installed.

The Churchward 2-6-0s, still in limited production, provided the GWR with much of its mixed traffic motive power, yet the Operating Department often rostered them for quite demanding heavy goods or semi-fast passenger work. Such tasks were putting these moderately sized locomotives to the limit of their powers. Clearly something needed to be done to satisfy the increasing train loads demanded. The first suggestion was to provide a design based on a modified Mogul, by replacing the pony truck with a leading bogie and fitting a standard No. 1 boiler. However, this proposal received short shrift from Collett, who was of the opinion that a modification of the existing 'Saint' class, employing smaller driving wheels, would be more appropriate. This was communicated to the drawing office, which speedily produced a diagram. The engine that resulted was basically a 'Saint' with 6 ft coupled wheels and a side window cab similar to that of the 'Castle'.

Accordingly, in 1924, No. 2925 *Saint Martin*, was withdrawn and modified for trials, which lasted a total of three years. This prototype for the '4900', or 'Hall' class proved a most capable design and, following completion of the assessment, a production batch of 80 was authorised in 1928, with a total of 259 being constructed through to 1943. This was not to be the end, as Hawksworth was to continue production of a further 71 in a modified form, until 1950.

Yet another winner, destined for virtually continuous production to almost the end of steam, had been turned out using Collett's engineering expertise. His name was most certainly becoming associated with production longevity.

The 'Hall' class was, perhaps, the most versatile locomotive designed under Collett. It proved so good that when Stanier departed for the job of CME on the LMS, he answered their need for a new and powerful mixed-traffic type by specifying an LMS-styled 'Hall' class to fill the need. This was his class '5' 4-6-0, or 'Black Five', of which no fewer than 842 were eventually built.

Problems, for Collett, were to be analysed deeply, sometimes in discussion with those immediately below him. However, the final decision always came from himself. In this way he was able to search out those persons likely to be considered for future high office and, eventually, to be short-listed as a potential major assistant. His naturally quiet manner hid a perceptive mind which continuously looked ahead for the future deployment of his officers and staff.

Quite often Churchward would walk along the track from Newburn House and cross over to the design block, to meet up with some of his old colleagues. He apparently called in to see Collett on many of these occasions, who never tried to restrict access to his former chief, after all he now held the reins and had a good legacy of sound designs on which to build. It could well have been that he welcomed the opportunity to talk matters over with the master and benefit from his experience.

In keeping with developments on other railways, the LMS in particular, the locomotive design team at Swindon started some studies into a 4-cylinder compound variant of the 'Castle' class. It was sensible, they reckoned, to follow trends elsewhere and be ready to move forward should the case for compound propulsion be made. Fowler on the LMS, taking his lead from Hughes before him, was engaged in the early production phases of a compound Pacific and had got to the stage of some component manufacture. So it seemed that a watching brief, in the shape of some diagrams, was required, in case the Locomotive Committee started asking why the GWR was not following suit. However Churchward's decisive series of tests in the early years of the century into compound versus simple locomotives, resulting in a clear advantage for the simple case, probably made Collett cautious in accepting so radical a change in design philosophy. Hawksworth, in charge of the locomotive drawing office, drafted out a diagram embodying 17 inch high pressure and 25 inch low pressure cylinders, the tractive effort being 35,700 lb., which was then taken by Stanier and himself into Collett's office. Five minutes later they came out, suitably chastened, and consigned the drawing to the waste bin! An incorporation of compounds would have gone against the standardisation policy built up over the years. The schemes thus got no further than the drawing board, being swiftly turned down by Collett when presented to him.

Apart from all these new developments, Swindon works were also engaged in turning out more batches of Churchward designs, these being the

No. 4940 *Ludford Hall* on a stopping passenger duty at Banbury *c*.1931.

R.S. Carpenter Collection

Stanier's 'Black Five' was strongly based on the 'Hall'. Here No. 5041 of that class prepares to leave Nottingham (Midland) on a semi-fast passenger turn in the mid-1930s.

John Scott-Morgan Collection

No 4920 *Dumbleton Hall* rests at Old Oak Common, September 1934. This locomotive has been preserved and is to be found on the South Devon Railway in fine fettle.

R.S. Carpenter Collection

A Bournemouth to Birkenhead train is headed by No. 4924 *Eydon Hall* in 1931, as it approaches Banbury. The stock appears to be of Southern Railway origin. *R.S. Carpenter Collection*

An unidentified 'Hall' class with a 4,000 gallon tender, leaves Dainton tunnel with a Newton Abbot-bound local. c.1938.

John Scott-Morgan Collection

Collett's 'Hall' class was a genuine mixed-traffic type. No. 5977 *Beckford Hall* on a Cardiff -Birmingham express passes Malvern Wells. *c.*1945.   *John Scott-Morgan Collection*

No. 4943 *Marrington Hall* is being banked up to Dainton tunnel with a down freight *c.*1948.
                                                          John Scott-Morgan Collection

No. 4982 *Acton Hall* on a down express near Dainton tunnel. *c.*1947-8.
John Scott-Morgan Collection

Eleven of the 'Hall' class were fitted out for oil burning in 1946-7, and renumbered into the '3900' series. Here No. 3955 *Haberfield Hall*, formerly No. 6949, is found at Plymouth Laira in August 1948.   *R.S. Carpenter Collection*

'4500'/'4575' class 2-6-2T, the '5205' class 2-8-0T and more of the '4300' class 2-6-0 to fill the needs of local passenger and freight workings, which were rapidly becoming too much for the older types. Meantime, the drawing office was working on two new designs, a 0-6-2T for the South Wales lines and a further express development of the 'Castles'. The tank is covered in the appropriate chapter and our next assessment of Collett's expertise is to cover the development of perhaps the most important GWR express locomotive, the 'King' class.

But first, a short digression involving the 'Castle' class is appropriate. The performance of the 'Castles' was becoming legendary and, following the 1925 exchange with the LNER, a further exchange came about, this time with the LMS. This particular event was primarily to enable the LMS to run a 'Castle' on its Euston to Carlisle expresses to aid the railway in assessing whether a locomotive of its power was suitable. The LMS CME's department at Derby was bypassed for this exchange, the initial suggestion apparently coming from the GWR General Manager, Sir Felix Pole, who was a close friend of the LMS Chairman, Sir Guy Granet, to 'try one of ours'. Derby could quite easily have given a considered opinion on the locomotive power and size needed, indeed, Fowler's Pacific designs mentioned earlier had only just been scrapped after some manufacture had commenced. Fowler, already smarting after that event, must have been somewhat annoyed at this bypassing of his department, but graciously accepted what the LMS Board had instigated, not wishing to upset the status quo. He even provided a compound 4-4-0 for trials on the GWR.

No. 5000 *Launceston Castle* was dispatched to the LMS and immediately showed itself to be capable of meeting all the trials' requirements, which were carried out complete with dynamometer car.

The net result of the LMS test programme was a request to the GWR Board to consider supplying 50 'Castles'. Apart from this breaking the long-standing agreement between the UK railways which prevented them from selling their own products to others, Collett flatly refused to condone such a plan. It would lead to considerable disruption of the Swindon production schedules at a time when the works was at full stretch. This understandable refusal was then countered by a request for a full set of 'Castle' drawings. Charles Collett immediately let the Board know that this was completely against his policy of keeping the technological details of Swindon designs firmly within the confines of his department. The Board was persuaded to agree with him and the LMS was duly informed of its decision.

In the latter respect of drawings, Sir Henry Fowler turned from the GWR to the Southern with much greater effect, obtaining a set of drawings of Maunsell's 'Lord Nelson' 4-6-0, which incorporated many Swindon ideas, and the ensuing programme of development resulting in the 'Royal Scot' class is legendary in railway history. Charles sat back in some relief after letting his staff know that they were to remain cautious as to information which may be supplied to other railways.

Although Collett would have attended some of the ARLE meetings during the past three years, there is no mention of him participating in any discussion. Matters at Swindon were very busy and he was much in demand

Southern Railway Maunsell 'Lord Nelson' class 4-6-0 No. 850 *Lord Nelson* himself, at Stewart's Lane *c*.1930.   *R.S. Carpenter Collection*

LMS 'Royal Scot' class 4-6-0 No. 6112 *Sherwood Forester* and its crew pose for the photographer in this view taken at Camden.   *John Alsop Collection*

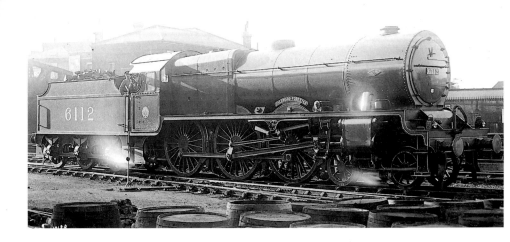

masterminding the busy programme of new locomotive design and production schedules. A GWR representation at the ARLE was now restricted to the occasional appearance of Collett, a far cry from the days when Churchward was CME and much involved in affairs. The wartime design committee for standard locomotives had been strongly supported by Churchward as a forum, to impress on other CMEs his preferred design features, which offered increased performance commensurate with economy. Although Collett had gathered an extremely competent team under him at Swindon, he felt unable to delegate much outside contract work where technical design matters were concerned, preferring to be closely involved himself. In fact, we have already seen he was never very amenable to his staff visiting other railway works on engineering matters. These last were strictly in-house at Swindon, the general GWR thinking being that anything outside its works was not quite up to its standards.

There was, however, one episode which went against this last statement, in that during 1925 the GWR had the opportunity of acquiring a 'foreign' locomotive in the shape of 80 ex-Ministry of Transport Robinson 2-8-0s offered for purchase at £1,500 each. They were in a general state of disrepair, so after a few weeks in use Collett had them taken out of service and thoroughly checked as to their condition. Thirty proved to be suitable to undergo a rebuild, the remaining 50 being given a brief overhaul before returning to traffic and run until further upkeep became uneconomic. Many of the rebuilt engines lasted through to Nationalisation, but the 50 given the minimum attention were all gone by 1931. With the GWR 2-8-0 costing some £7,000, it made economic sense to supplant their work by these cheap additions, which did not dig too deep into the limited funds available for new stock.

Matters in the CME's department had been far from smooth over the first three years of Charles Collett's tenure of office as CME, for the drawing office underwent two changes at the top due to totally unforeseen circumstances. Collett most certainly had some quick and decisive decisions to make in promoting his staff into vacant positions to ensure that the job of chief draughtsman was in capable hands at a critical time for the locomotive developments he had planned for the GWR.

Churchward's chief draughtsman from 1905 was G.H. Burrows, who had been actively involved in the standard locomotive programme following his successful tenure as a senior draughtsman during the Dean/Churchward transition. According to some contemporary reports he was not popular with some staff, but his handling of the matters affected by the delicate balance of power as Dean's mental state grew ever more precarious, and Churchward gradually assumed more authority, was enough to get him promoted in 1905.

An efficent chief, he covered his responsibilities adequately enough to be left in charge when Collett became CME. However, he died suddenly in 1923, as Collett was beginning to assert his authority, at the age of just 53. His successor was O.E.F. Deverell, who had been the leading draughtsman responsible for Churchward's second prototype 4-6-0, No. 98, which formed the start of the 'Saint' class. Deverell's efforts on this keystone design, which incorporated many of the Churchward features to be carried through by Collett, were rewarded by promotion to assistant chief draughtsman in 1907. However,

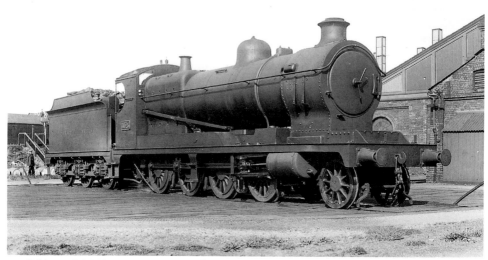

Robinson 2-8-0 No. 3025 at Reading Shed on 17th May, 1935. The GWR rebuilds included the safety valve bonnet and the top-feed.   *R.S. Carpenter Collection*

One of the Robinson 2-8-0s that stood the test of time on the GWR. No. 3011 was still in service in the 1950s.   *R.S. Carpenter Collection*

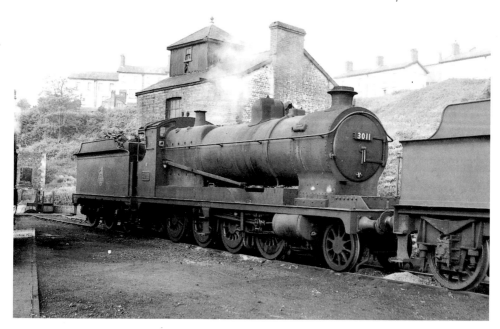

Collett hardly had time to get his programme under way when, in 1925, Deverell himself died. He was only 50.

F.W. Hawksworth, later to become Collett's successor as CME, took Deverell's place and was speedily established enabling the staffing at last to be steadied for the important days that lay ahead, as the final express locomotive development to come from Collett was being formulated. The development of this, the 'King' class, is covered in the following chapter.

Hawksworth had been noted as one of the potential high-flyers in the locomotive drawing office and early on in Collett's time as CME, he and Stanier had discussed his situation. Stanier had suggested that a time in top management, as Works Manager, would be useful to further his career. Collett, however, said that he could not be spared from the drawing office as so many of the new design responsibilities passed through him. And so R.A.G. Hannington was appointed Locomotive Works Manager, a choice which was to prove very beneficial.

In the context of the need to improve the repair costs of locomotive stock, some discussion was held with the new Works Manager and his immediate staff surrounding the calling-in for general repairs, which constituted a complete disassembly and rebuild to 'as new' condition. At the best of times this was an expensive exercise, absorbing much of the maintenance budget.

When Charles Collett became CME the average mileage run between shopping for general repairs was some 80,000. In order to try and reduce the outlay needed to cover the cost of shopping at this interval it was suggested to him by his senior works staff that an extension to this mileage could be achieved by calling in a locomotive for a relatively minor 'Intermediate' repair at some 60,000 miles. This 'I' repair involved leaving the boiler on the frames with probably some tubes being replaced and concentrating on tyres, axleboxes, pistons and motion, all relatively inexpensive to deal with. This would allow the locomotive to cover a further 60,000 miles before needing to resort to a general repair. Therefore general repairs were spaced at 120,000 miles and hence reduced frequency. The saving in cost was considerable even after allowing for the intermediate repair expenses.

As experience with this new scheme grew, in later years it was possible to schedule two, or even three, intermediate repairs to some classes, thereby extending the mileage further between general repairs with over 250,000 miles becoming possible.

Chapter Seven

The 'King' Class Development

As the design office began to translate Collett's orders into a new prestige express locomotive, the GWR Social and Educational Union held its fourth annual music festival. Although he normally shunned involvement in outside interests, Charles Collett was persuaded, on the odd occasion, to come out of his shell and accepted the offer to chair this event, which took place at Swindon in February 1927. This was a rare public appearance for him which was mentioned in a positive sense by Sir Felix Pole in his speech at the opening. Considerable applause accompanied this statement which clearly indicated the esteem in which Collett was held.

The festival, according to contemporary accounts, was organised with its usual excellence and, in his closing remarks at the end of the competitions, Charles Collett made some interesting and inspiring remarks, following which he was given appropriate musical honours by some of the competitors.

To assist him in the distribution of the awards, Charles had the help of Mrs Stanier at the close of the proceedings. The notable feature of this participation was that it drew from Collett a letter to the *GWR Magazine* concerning one of the competitions, that on Public Speaking. Letters from him on subjects other than railways are rare and this one is quoted in full here:

Dear Sir,
  Among the many interesting things that took place at the Festival, one of the items that struck me was the phrase chosen for one of the competitions: 'Procrastination is the Thief of Time'. I append some notes setting out my views on the subject.
  Yours faithfully
      C.B. Collett

Procrastination is delay.
A thief is a person who steals.
Procrastination should have been compared to Stealing, or a Procrastinator to a Thief.
Time is duration, and the basis of its measurement on this earth is the period occupied by this planet in travelling one complete circuit around the sun.
We are each allotted a portion of time - our lifetime - every moment of which we have to live and are responsible for.
We can employ our time usefully or otherwise, but we can neither lose nor find nor give time, and it certainly cannot be taken from us.
Even the thief who is cast into prison has to 'do time' there.
Our time, however, comes to an end, and this occurs when our soul departs from our mortal body, and we are then faced with the great Eternity, from whence we came at birth.
Therefore, I say, that Procrastination cannot be a thief, and Time cannot be stolen.

This letter and its contents show a precise and analytical person who was also very aware of something existing outside this life on earth, but a little hesitant in specifying exactly what that something is.

The new express engine mentioned above was to become the renowned 'King' class, but before launching into the story of its birth, some qualifying remarks need to be made.

For many years the compartmental make-up of GWR disciplines had resulted in a distinct lack of communication between departments. As Churchward, followed by Collett, had produced designs for progressively larger and heavier locomotives, the Civil Engineer's Department had been carrying out an upgrade to 22 tons axle loading, of the track and bridges on the main lines. However, this had not been communicated to the CME's Department which was still working to the old 19½ ton limit in 1926.

Pole and Sir Aubrey Brocklebank, a Director who took a considerable interest in locomotive practice, often found time to discuss railway matters between themselves. Brocklebank, who had an estate in Cumberland through which ran the 15 inch gauge Ravenglass & Eskdale Railway, the building of which he had actively encouraged, had some small criticisms of the 'Castle' class. Pole took advantage of a meeting with Collett on locomotive matters to raise the question of axle loading which was, at that time, still restricted to 19 tons. The 'Castles' had been designed right up to this loading. Collett mentioned that it was this limit that hampered locomotive practice and development on the GWR, remarking: 'If I could have an axle loading of 22½ tons, I would give you a very fine locomotive'.

At a future meeting between Pole and Brocklebank in 1926, at which the limiting features in railway affairs were discussed, the limit of the main line carrying capacity was brought up. Brocklebank suggested that a possible restriction could be brought about by the bridges, and suggested that a table be prepared to show the maximum axle load for each bridge. Pole agreed that this would be useful and called in Lloyd, the Chief Civil Engineer. Lloyd agreed to this request and was about to leave the room, when Pole asked: 'By the way, Mr Lloyd, when designing new bridges, for what axle load do you provide?' Lloyd replied: 'Twenty-two tons'. It transpired that this value had been in operation for over 22 years, having been recommended to the Engineering Committee of the Board by Sir James Inglis in his time as Chief Civil Engineer.

Inglis, who died at the early age of 61 in 1911, had been a far-seeing man and on very good terms with Churchward and no doubt both had come to an agreement that a heavier axle loading on bridges would be advantageous in the future. However, although Inglis had gone ahead with the larger 22 ton limit on all future bridge renewals from that time, he completely neglected to inform Churchward formally and, for that matter, any department outside of his own. But then he had been promoted to General Manager in 1903, just after his discussion with Churchward who, at that time, was deeply involved in starting on his standardisation programme and the matter clearly drifted from his mind.

Further questioning by Pole revealed the fact that these bridges conforming to this 22 ton limit had sufficient reserve strength to accept a 22½ ton axle load, and only four bridges required renewing on the West of England main line to accept this load. Pole issued an order that the remaining bridges be rebuilt immediately and contacted Collett with the following order: 'You can build a new locomotive having an axle load of 22½ tons, and we will have it for the

The event and location are unknown, but this photograph depicts 'King' class No. 6029 *King Stephen* alongside a Southern Railway 'Lord Nelson' class locomotive. On the left can be seen the corridor tender of a Gresley Pacific. Judging by the pristine condition of the engines this was at some form of exhibition.   *R.S. Carpenter Collection*

A particularly good photograph depicting the clean lines of the King class. No. 6022 *King Edward VI* at Old Oak Common in 1933.   *R.S. Carpenter Collection*

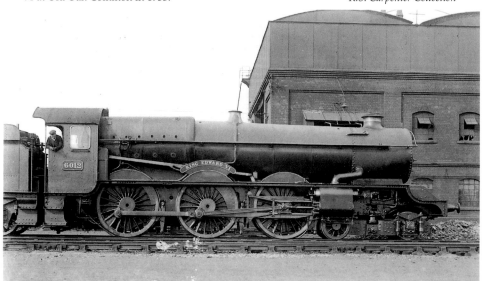

summer traffic next year'. He also specified a tractive effort of at least 40,000 lb. This last specification stemmed from the fact that R.E.L. Maunsell's new 4-6-0, the 'Lord Nelson' class, was advertised as having a tractive effort of 33,500 lb., thus claiming to be 'the most powerful passenger engine in the UK'. The 'Castle' class had been displaced from its top placing and the GWR Publicity Department was keen to get this title back with a sufficient margin unlikely to be bettered by other railways for some years. (In fact, this value for British express types was never to be exceeded to the end of steam, but was equalled by the Stanier 'Princess Royal' Pacific on the LMS in 1934.) It was also a good advertisement for the railway, particularly as the 'Lord Nelson' was likely to be used on the competitive Southern Railway West of England services.

The locomotive that ensued from this directive, at first known as the 'Super-Castle', was the 'King' or '6000' class. It represented a new approach in design techniques with the need to keep the overall weight to an acceptable level. After all, the axle loading rise would only allow for a total weight increase of 7½ tons in adhesive weight. For instance, the boiler was a 'special' of 6 ft maximum diameter, the No. 7 standard boiler of this diameter as used on the 2-8-0s being too heavy. The bogie also needed a peculiar cranked frame necessitated by clearance with the forward-mounted inside cylinders. Also the driving wheels departed from the standard 6 ft 8½ in. normally used on all express locomotives to 6 ft 6 in. This last feature was dictated purely by the personal whim of Collett, although it has been stated elsewhere that the smaller diameter was to achieve the 40,000 lb. tractive effort. This is not so, for in the original study, with the 6 ft 6 in. wheels, the tractive effort was 39,100 lb. and employed a 16 inch cylinder diameter. The 40,300 lb. tractive effort of the final design was, in fact, decided by increasing the cylinder diameter by ¼ inch to 16¼ inches.

The 6 ft 6 in. driving wheel diameter, non-standard, followed an experience Collett had which helped him decide on this value as being suitable. He and C.C. Crump, by now the Running Superintendent, were travelling to Paddington on an express which, at one point on the journey, was overtaken by a train hauled by a class '4300' Mogul with its 5 ft 8 in. wheels. Crump was all for reprimanding the driver of the Mogul, having taken the number of the locomotive, but was dissuaded from doing so by Collett, as he explained: 'This confirms a thought I have had recently'.

Shortly after this Collett ordered that a 'Castle' class be modified to test a 6 ft 6 in. wheel. No. 5002 *Ludlow Castle*, had its tyres turned down to 6 ft 6 in. and was put back into service. The effect on performance was negligible, which satisfied Collett that this diameter was perfectly acceptable for fast express use, despite the fact that it departed from a long-established standard.

In this rather round-about way to meet the requirements, this departure from a standard feature was to bring about an expensive locomotive, but then prestige was involved in terms of perceived power. Collett and his team dealt well with a tricky situation on the design side, and the works coped well with a tight time schedule for the construction of a largely non-standard locomotive demanded of them. For it transpired that in August 1927 the prototype would be in the USA, participating in the Baltimore & Ohio Railroad centenary celebrations, the President of that line having thought it appropriate to have an English engine

'King' class 4-6-0 No. 6023 *King Edward II* rests at Kingswear in the early 1930s, before being turned for the return journey.   *R.S. Carpenter Collection*

No 6015 *King Richard III* arrives at Torre with a Paddington-Kingswear express in the late 1930s.
John Scott-Morgan Collection

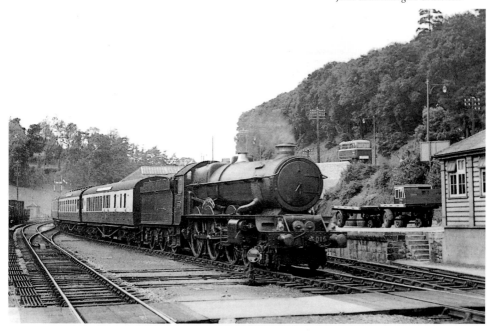

taking part. He communicated this to Sir Felix Pole through an associate at the Stockton & Darlington centenary parade that followed the 1925 International Railway Congress. As the design began to take shape, Pole, realising that the new GWR express locomotive should be available in 1927, immediately decided that this would be the engine to go to America. All the stops were out at Swindon in the first half of 1927, and the prototype, No. 6000, was turned out in June 1927, receiving the name *King George V*, beating Fowler's *Royal Scot* which had been derived from Maunsell's *Lord Nelson* by almost a month.

In order that No. 6000 was fully run-in before dispatch to the USA, after the usual light running-in turns were completed it was put on the down 'Cornish Riviera Express' or 'Limited' from Paddington to Plymouth. Performance was creditable with, for the first time ever, on a regular basis, a load of nearly 350 tons being taken over the steep grades of South Devon without any banking assistance. Within a few weeks five more 'Kings' had entered service, and were coping with equivalent or greater loads with equal ability.

Collett delegated Stanier to accompany the locomotive to the USA, where after the centenary displays it was agreed that it would be available to undertake some trial running on the Baltimore & Ohio Railroad (B&ORR) between Baltimore and Philadelphia. However, before this run was due to take place, Stanier had received a cable from Collett in which it was ordered that no main line running should take place until a modification to the bogie springing had been carried out. The cause of this modification stemmed from an incident at Midgham, where the 'Cornish Riviera Express' had been halted following the derailment of the bogie of No. 6003. Collett had, on hearing of this derailment, called one of his staff in and, grabbing an umbrella, said: 'Come on, we have some investigating to do'.

Arriving at the scene of the accident, Collett proceeded to march down the track along which the express had travelled, until he came to the point where the bogie wheel flange marks could be seen on the rail top. Walking a few yards further he proceeded to poke at the sleepers with the point of his umbrella. Several sleepers were soft, permitting the point to penetrate. Subsequent tests on the bogie springing showed that a rail deflection of just 1½ inches relieved the front bogie wheel of all load. At the subsequent enquiry, he managed to pass the blame onto the Civil Engineer on the grounds of the track being defective.

There had been other derailments on the GWR that year, it having been an abnormally wet year with the track suffering from localised water-logged conditions. A 2-6-2T, No. 4508, had been derailed near Kidderminster and a Mogul had partially derailed, the leading coupled wheels leaving the rails, in Cornwall. So, armed with the evidence of these events and his own findings at Midgham, Charles was able to make a good case citing the track condition as being the culprit, rather than exhuberant driving or springing deficiencies in his locomotives. His sway with the Locomotive Committee at Paddington also helped smooth over what could have been an embarrassing incident for his Department. The Southern Railway had not been so lucky, for its derailment at Sevenoaks, caused partially by the effect of heavy rain on the trackbed, had resulted in 13 deaths and the inquiry that ensued poured blame on both locomotive and track.

'King' class No. 6007 *King William III* on an up 'Cornish Riviera Express' passes Coryton Cove near Dawlish. c.1938. This was the locomotive badly damaged in the Shrivenham disaster and subsequently rebuilt.

R.S. *Carpenter Collection*

To return to the bogie problems, the springing of the front axle was, following the deflection tests, softened by introducing coil springs on the spring hangers. The task of designing the modifications required was given to A.W.J. Dymond, a young draughtsman who had been transferred to Swindon from the drawing office at the Taff Vale works at Grouping. This modification was transmitted to Stanier in Baltimore who immediately arranged for the changes to be carried out on No. 6000 in the workshops of the B&ORR, before the main line tests commenced. The modifications satisfactorily carried out, the locomotive then took a test train on an extensive tour which was satisfactorily completed with complete reliability hauling the train of nearly 550 tons at speeds equivalent to the American locomotives then in use.

As the foundation of the 'King' class was being laid there was yet another intake of Premium Apprentices being considered. Their fee was £100, which was, as usual, a perk for the CME, for a five-year apprenticeship at the Works. The decision as to their acceptance came from the CME himself. Although rarely, if ever, seeing the established Premium Apprentices - except at their initial interview, Collett did take an interest in their progress so far as their technical education was concerned. For instance, after the first year evening class attendances and end of year examinations, the top 15 were given one day a week release to study for their National Certificates. They were also given encouragement to add to these studies by taking extra classes for a Whitworth Scholarship and the External Intermediate qualification of the University of London. Those few who succeeded, in these higher achievements could then be given leave to attend the Mechanical Engineering BSc (Eng.) course at Imperial College, with the condition that they returned to Swindon during all the vacation periods for practical experience in the Shops. His own attendance at the City and Guilds, which by this time had been absorbed into Imperial College, probably led Collett to realise the benefits of higher education to Degree standard and permit this.

ARLE matters were sparse in 1928, only two meetings that year, the first of which saw Charles Collett elected as President at the February gathering, taking the chair for that event. He is not recorded as having attended the second, July, meeting. However, at the following year's January meeting he was there, and at this gathering some agreement on a standard locomotive tyre flange depth was reached. The depth settled was 1½ inches, with a wear limit of 1⅛ inches depth. Charles Collett, however, in view of his still present worries brought about by the spate of derailments on the GWR 18 months previously, thought long and hard about the new standard. He enquired of the drawing office and maintenance staff as to the feasibility of taking the starting depth as 1⁵⁄₁₆ inches. He was given assurances that, under normal wear conditions, the depth would not reach the limit before the engines were due for shopping, and accordingly ordered that this revised value was henceforth to be taken as a standard. In this decision he was supported by the Chief Inspecting Officer of the Ministry of Transport. The other railways, via their respective CMEs, were unwilling to change to it, having agreed to adopt the ARLE standard. Collett stuck to his decision and refused to depart from it. In later years, after Nationalisation, this Swindon policy was to remain and caused some degree of troubles when rationalising production methodology on BR.

No. 6003 *King George IV* at Old Oak Common. *c.*1948 with 'BRITISH RAILWAYS' shown on the
tender.   *R.S. Carpenter/L.W. Perkins Collection*

Collett's 4-6-0 'King' class No. 6018 *King Henry VI* arrives at Lapworth with a
Birmingham-Leamington local on 25th April, 1963. Clearly this is a substitution, as No. 6018 was
withdrawn in late 1962, but retained and steamed when required.
                                                                    R.S. Carpenter/Joe Moss Collection

Despite his intermittent attendance at the ARLE proceedings, Charles did still make fairly regular forays to Waterloo to see R.E.L. Maunsell, who was a great user of Swindon design features on his locomotives, in which he was influenced by his Works Manager, George Pearson and Technical Assistant, Harold Holcroft, both ex-Swindon. Gresley and Fowler were often present and the CMEs discussed matters of mutual interest in Maunsell's office. Notably, only affable Sir Henry Fowler bothered to look in on the Assistants after seeing Maunsell, both Nigel Gresley and Charles Collett marching off without seemingly wanting to spend a few minutes with those key personnel, even though Collett, in particular, had known, and worked with, the ex-Swindon people in their GWR days.

So far as the GWR express locomotives were concerned, a total of 30 'Kings' were constructed, and were destined to remain the premier express type through into the BR Western Region days whilst steam remained.

The 'Kings', although proving powerful and reliable in service, did show some problems in the motion, due to what transpired to be slight wear in the operating levers for the outside valves. This resulted in some uneven steam distribution between outer and inner cylinders. Indicator trials in 1931 showed this up as a problem and the drawing office set to and schemed a modified lever to minimise this. S.O. Ell was the draughtsman involved. Charles Collett, however, when presented with the scheme flatly refused to accept it, not wishing to instigate any changes at this stage. He was quite happy to continue using the motion originally designed. After all, it was based on the Churchward original.

The above happened just before Stanier left for the LMS and it is notable that he insisted on four sets of valve motion for his first Pacifics, which guaranteed good steam distribution. Only when he had rearranged his design team at Derby to his satisfaction did he switch to two sets of valve gear, following Ell's concept, for the later series of Pacifics.

One final comment on the 'Kings' is worthy of note here. In 1935, Collett received a note from Stanier, now well-established on the LMS. In this note was the revelation that the application of low-degree superheat on the LMS was not particularly successful and in the investigations to try and overcome the short-comings, it had been noticed that the area for the passage of steam through the 14-element superheater tubes was less than the area of the main steam pipe from the regulator. Stanier had been led to this by his attention being brought to continually low steam chest pressures. On changing to a 28-element superheater a dramatic change in performance had ensued. Maybe the 'Kings' might be improved by a similar change, for their superheaters were of similar format to the early low-degree ones, suggested Stanier.

Collett read the note, ascertained that no complaints about adverse performance were abroad, and ignored the advice. It was to remain for Hawksworth to take this on board some 12 years later, and make an excellent locomotive become outstanding in its final few years of service.

In 1938 a proposal to fit a Kylchap exhaust to the 'King' class was suggested to Collett. Other CMEs were experimenting with this modification, particularly Gresley on the LNER (it was the streamlined 'A4' Pacific *Mallard*, fitted with the Kylchap system and double chimney, that gained the World speed record of 126 mph in 1938). However, the proposal was rejected outright by Collett, he did not want any change in the status quo.

Many of the more serviceable 0-6-2Ts found in Wales at Grouping were rebuilt with standard boilers and gave many more years reliable service. No. 378 (ex-Taff Vale Railway No. 156) is found on shed at Treherbert on 27th March, 1939.   *R.S. Carpenter Collection*

Ex-Rhymney Railway 0-6-2T No. 38 after being given the Swindon treatment became GWR No. 81 at Caerphilly works, 27th March, 1939.   *R.S. Carpenter Collection*

Chapter Eight

Tanks and Small Mixed-Traffic Developments

Whilst all the express and mixed traffic developments were going on, Collett did not neglect that most ordinary of locomotives, the tank engine. Most of the GWR's shunting, local branch passenger and light freight work was catered for by such locomotives, mostly of the 0-6-0 type. There were some deviations from this wheel arrangement for these and specific other duties outside the ones listed above.

For example, much of the locomotive stock of the smaller, largely South Wales, railways taken over at Grouping, was in a very run down condition and needed replacement. The war had obviously affected maintenance and the supply of new locomotives and so one of the first tasks falling upon the CME's department at Swindon was to decide how to rectify the needs.

Firstly Collett ordered a complete survey of all the locomotives of these railways, from which he decided which would be scrapped and which were suitable for overhaul or rebuild. He requested the drawing office to investigate which of the standard boilers might be suitable as replacement items. In fact, it turned out that so many locomotives were involved it proved practical to modify three of the standard boilers so that a relatively large proportion of the inherited locomotives could be treated thus. This had the effect of permitting much of the repair work to be concentrated at Swindon, and allowed a reduction in the maintenance facilities in South Wales, thereby reducing costs. The predominant type found in South Wales was the 0-6-2T, the better of which were overhauled, many receiving a new Swindon boiler and sundry other fittings in the process. The scrapping of many others, he realised, would produce a severe motive power shortage, and ordered the drawing office to scheme an equivalent 0-6-2T to replace the condemned stock. In a break with the by now normal Swindon tradition of outside cylinders for medium to large sized locomotives, it was decided to keep to the inside cylinder format commonplace in Wales, the restricted loading gauge on those lines demanding this layout.

The '5600' class, as they were known, that resulted proved powerful and popular, being used on both passenger and freight work. Some 200 were built between 1924 and 1928, 50 of them by Armstrong Whitworth, as Swindon works was at full capacity with the new express types and the servicing and rebuilding of the best of the absorbed stock as 1927 approached. It was rare for new GWR locomotives to be built by an outside contractor, but Collett was not averse to using their facilities in time of urgent need, as this most certainly was. Recourse to outside contractors was entered into mainly because the Government of the day encouraged such measures under a scheme to relieve the unemployment situation. The Armstrong Whitworth order was, in fact, a particularly good placement, as its quote was very competitive and, once production was under way, the tanks were delivered at a steady rate of five per week.

The prototype '5600' class tank had a shaky start, as a failure occurred during the initial steaming test. This failure has only been reported correctly once, in Chapter Eleven of Gibson's treatise on GWR locomotive design. It is worth reporting here, as it gives an assessment of Collett's engineering expertise so far as new design is concerned.

The 0-6-2T was Collett's first, and only, design concocted from scratch. Although the basis of this locomotive was the Rhymney Railway 'R' class 0-6-2T, so far as wheelbase and general proportions were considered, the detail design was all Swindon. Many of the components used came from the stock of standard parts but, being of inside cylinder layout, new cylinders had to be provided. The piston valves were placed above the cylinders and this necessitated connection of the valve spindle to the extension rod. Normally, this would be done via a rock-shaft mounted in a substantial bearing if the engine was outside-cylindered. This bearing was capable of taking substantial side loads. The inside cylinder layout meant that the draughtsman given the job of laying out the motion connected the extension rod directly to the end of the valve spindle. The angular inclination of the rod meant that there was considerable up-thrust on the end of the spindle, particularly when everything was new and stiff.

With the drawing office at full stretch, somehow this bit of bad design slipped by both the chief draughtsman, O.E.F. Deverell, and Collett. Deverell had only been in office a few months, but that is no excuse for this lapse. The sheer pressure of work seems the likely culprit. The resulting failure occurred during the first steaming trial within the works' confines. With all ready, everything oiled, the boiler at or near maximum pressure, the regulator was opened by the trials' driver, and the engine moved off. Suddenly, with a grinding noise, the exhaust beats grew uneven and the regulator was shut and the engine halted. The upthrust on the unsupported end of the valve spindle had been sufficient to bend it and restrict its movement, thus producing the uneven exhaust beat.

This failure occurred in December 1924, just four months after the issue of the working drawings, and a further batch of tanks was approaching completion in 'A' shop. Such was the urgency for these engines that Collett had gone for series production immediately - no prototype. There was thus an immediate problem which needed sorting out quickly. And here we come across a piece of evidence which does suggest some degree of a cover-up operation.

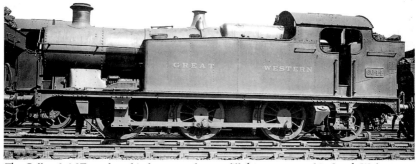

The Collett 0-6-2T produced in large numbers to fill the urgent need in South Wales were useful engines and were to be found in many other areas. Here we see No. 6644 in December 1930.   *John Alsop Collection*

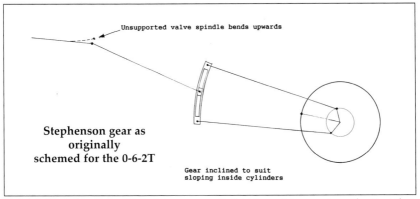

Unsupported valve spindle bends upwards

**Stephenson gear as
originally
schemed for the 0-6-2T**

Gear inclined to suit
sloping inside cylinders

After some hours to think things over, Collett issued two orders, the first that the staff responsible in the drawing office were not to leave their boards before a solution had been worked out. The second, and more devious, was that no one was to mention the happening on pain of instant dismissal. Collett had a reputation to keep up and had no wish to see that eroded by one piece of bad engineering.

A solution speedily appeared from the drawing office in the form of a massive cross-frame bridging the frames over the valve spindle ends. To this were fitted extension rod guides bolted under the cross member. The whole assembly was a rushed job and made the valve motion very inaccessible, but there were no reports of sackings and the cover-up was completed by dating the new drawings of December 1924 modifications as August 1924!

Never again did Collett order a brand-new design to be schemed, he stuck firmly to derivatives or enlargements of existing types from now on and stayed resolutely with Churchward's advanced concepts.

As first thoughts were being given to the needs of South Wales, it became apparant that there were certain areas which needed urgent action. In 1926 some 0-4-0Ts inherited from one of the smaller railways, the Swansea Harbour Trust, were in such bad repair that scrapping was the only answer. A replacement fleet of similar-sized locomotives was needed and, rather than place the design task with his hard-pressed design team, Collett placed an order for six 0-4-0Ts to his specification, on the Avonside Engine Company. These were the only steam locomotives to be designed and built by a private company for the GWR in the 20th century. The six examples were delivered in that year and served as dock shunters through into the 1960s.

Churchward's standardisation programme had not been comprehensive enough to include the more humble 0-6-0T, even though the GWR used them extensively for shunting and light freight work throughout the system. The existing Dean/Armstrong variants, the last examples built in 1896, were wearing out and replacements and additions were needed.

Collett ordered that the drawing office draw up a modernised version of the 1896, '2700' class as modified with pannier tanks. The resulting '5700' locomotive had a 200 psi Belpaire boiler, improved valve settings, larger bunker and a fully enclosed cab, otherwise it was as for the '2700' class. Mass production commenced in 1929 with the first 300 being built by outside contractors again using the Government support scheme. The remainder of the class, which totalled 863 by the time production ceased in 1950, came from Swindon.

'1101' class 0-4-0T, an Avonside design, is found here at Danygraig in the early 1930s.
John Scott-Morgan Collection

A clutch of 0-6-0PTs rest at Bristol St Philip's Marsh in the 1920s. The central outside-framed
example, No. 1149, is Armstrong '1076' 'Buffalo' class.   *R.S. Carpenter Collection*

An Armstrong class '2021' 0-6-0PT which was the basis for Collett's class '5700'. Here No. 2079, still with half-cab, is found at Bristol St Philip's Marsh in the 1920s. *R.S. Carpenter Collection*

Churchward began to rebuild the '1701' class 0-6-0STs as 0-6-0PTs from 1912. Here No. 1799 is found at Truro in 1948. Compare this with the Collett '5700' class and it is obvious where the basic design came from. *R.S. Carpenter/Joe Moss Collection*

The '5700' class 0-6-0PT was in production from 1929 to 1950, a total of 863 being produced. This one, No. 3770, was turned out at Swindon in 1938 and is seen here on a pick-up freight run in 1939 approaching Sonning cutting.   *John Scott-Morgan Collection*

Earlier batches of the '5700' class 0-6-0PT had a simpler cab design than the later batches. No. 5741 at Newport Ebbw Junction on 30th July, 1939.   *R.S. Carpenter Collection*

The Churchward class '4500' 2-6-2T was produced under Collett in considerable numbers. Here one is on a substantial freight approaching Dainton tunnel. A banker is assisting. c.1946.   *John Scott-Morgan Collection*

A further tank locomotive to appear in 1929 was an extra batch of the Churchward 2-6-2T of the '3100' class. Collett made minimal changes to this 1903 standard design, and over his remaining time as CME 100 were built. Further batches of this design were to be built until 1949, such was their usefulness. So Churchward's legacy lived on for nearly 50 years as a standard production item! The standardisation programme planned all those years ago certainly proved that Churchward's foresight was absolutely correct.

Ever since his tragic loss of Ethelwyn in 1923 the events surrounding her fatal illness had affected Charles' thinking towards medical practices for, at some time after the dramatic change in his life, he apparently began to study reference books on medicine. Sometimes he would mention to his senior officers his thoughts on the current medical expertise, and was very critical of some practices. It was as though he was searching for a more plausible answer to his wife's passing than he had received fom her doctors. The recovery from this personal tragedy had been gradual, but definite, and his application to the job as CME recovered considerably, as witness the stream of successful designs to appear under his guidance, although he had never seemed the same man again.

In these later years he claimed to have cured himself from cancer by strict abstinence and dieting, but it is unclear as to whether this took place in the immediate months following Ethelwyn's passing, or at another, later, time. Be that as it may, according to contemporary accounts, he certainly became quite knowledgeable on medical matters in the latter years of his CME tenure.

However, the needs of the continued design and development programme had gradually brought about what seemed to be an almost complete recovery,

The '5100' class 2-6-2Ts were built to Churchward's design by Collett. This example, No. 5156, of the 1929 batch pilots a 'Castle' on a down express climbing Dainton Bank.

John Scott-Morgan Collection

Here 2-6-2T No. 6163 of the '6100' class built under Collett in 1935 is found on a Southampton-Reading service. Note the ex-LSWR stock employed in the 1930s.

John Scott-Morgan Collection

but in the background were the stirrings of an earnest search for some means of communication with his loved one. Always searching for answers to difficult problems, it was natural for Charles to consider anything he could find to try and bridge the gap between himself and Ethelwyn. Having studied psychical claims to this effect, he began to contact the relevant organisations to see what they had to offer, this interest growing into an obsession. His previous limited social life, built around his wife, was filled by an almost paranoic search for some means of getting in touch with her.

Many of those around him at work detected a clear change in attitudes caused by this growing obsession, but the old engineering and management skills remained and he had gradually got back into full sway as CME.

As the 1930s approached, rumours of experiments with diesel power on the railways overseas, particularly in Germany, were being reported into fact. The internal combustion engines, both petrol and diesel, were becoming reliable and economic with the private car and road lorry and buses growing in numbers as the years progressed. Even though the spectre of recession had appeared, investment in road transport was growing. The immediacy and convenience of these forms of transport was beginning to be felt in reduced receipts on the railways as more and more potential passengers switched to road.

Not wishing to be seen lacking in the advance of technology associated with the motive power of railways, the GWR Board asked Collett to consider the possibility of diesel traction, and a study of the potential of diesel multiple units and diesel locomotives for main and branch line work was carried out. Collett himself wrote much of the final report of this study, not finding much, in a positive sense, to support such a proposal.

He cited the steam locomotive as being very economical on fuel, stating that the 'Cornish Riviera Express' made its Paddington to Plymouth journey on four tons of coal, which at 17 shillings a ton was less than £4. However, he omitted to account for the cost of servicing at the turnround, plus the cost of maintaining water supplies *en route*. Neither were the substantial savings due to increased availability of the diesel, the potential for faster running times due to superior acceleration, or the general reduction in fixed plant such as engine sheds, workshops or water supply pumping gear accounted for.

Admittedly, the diesel was a relatively new power unit and, according to some contemporary reports, expensive to purchase, so perhaps he was correct in playing down the potential. However, he was eventually to revise his opinion within three years when a reasonably priced proposal from the Associated Engineering Company (AEC) at Southall was to catch his notice, as we shall see in Chapter Ten.

By 1929 the large numbers of 2-6-0s and 2-8-0s produced for goods traffic had resulted in the withdrawal and scrapping of large numbers of Armstrong and Dean 0-6-0s, which created a shortage of light 0-6-0s for use on the branch and absorbed lines. There were still a large number of Dean Goods 0-6-0s which were popular and reliable, despite their age. When some of these were dispatched to cover the shortfall caused by withdrawal of the older types a need grew to provide replacements to take over their main line duties.

The Dean Goods had been updated and improved by Collett, in fitting them with superheated Belpaire boilers and, as they were sent to their new duties, a

This 1940 build, of the '2251' class (No. 2220) shows the standard cab eventually fitted after the war. Seen at Cheddar. in 1948.   *J.H. Moss Collection*

Collett had been retired some three years when 0-6-0 No. 2239 was built. This photograph was taken at Oswestry in 1955 and indicates that cab modifications sometimes took a long time to appear.   *R.S. Carpenter Collection*

The batches of Collett 0-6-0s turned out during the war years had modified cab sidesheets without the side window. Here No. 2213 of 1940 is found on a Taunton-Minehead branch train in the late 1940s.   *John Scott-Morgan Collection*

replacement was designed. This was the '2251' class, or 'Collett Goods' as it eventually became known, a first batch of 20 being built in 1930. Much commonality with other designs was apparent, with the frames and motion that of the '5700' class tanks, the smokebox coming from the standard No. 10 boiler assembly and the boiler itself a modified standard No. 2.

This popular class was to remain in production until 1948 and acquired a reputation for steady running at speeds beyond 60 mph when employed on passenger work. Charles Collett had produced yet another versatile, reliable and long-lived locomotive to bolster the lighter duties of the mixed-traffic fleet.

With the undoubted success and popularity of the 0-6-0PT entering service it was natural to consider this layout for replacing more of the Victorian 0-6-0Ts used for auto-train work. As a reasonably powerful and speedy locomotive was needed for this work, a range of alternative designs were considered by Collett and the drawing office team. The 2-4-0T, 0-4-2T, 2-4-2T, 2-6-2T, 4-4-4T and 4-6-4T layouts were investigated. However, the 0-6-0PT kept coming back as the most cost-effective answer, with only the 0-4-2T approaching it in terms of overall performance and economy. Accordingly, Collett instructed that a variant of the Armstrong '2021' class 0-6-0T be schemed, with No. 2062 of that class rebuilt as a prototype in 1930 for trials whilst the production batch of 24 (the '5400' class) were manufactured.

Yet a further variation on the 0-6-0PT theme appeared a year later, the '6400' class, for light passenger work throughout the GWR. A large degree of commonality with the earlier Collett tanks was evident. Ninety were built, the first 40 fitted for auto-train working. Production of this type was to continue until 1950.

The work on tank engines continued unabated with the introduction of the '4800' class 0-4-2T in 1932. With this Collett produced a modern version of the old Armstrong '517' class, which proved to be an efficient machine, used mainly on branch line passenger work. So popular and useful they proved to be, that a total of 95 were eventually built (including the 20 non-auto-fitted engines of the '5800' series).

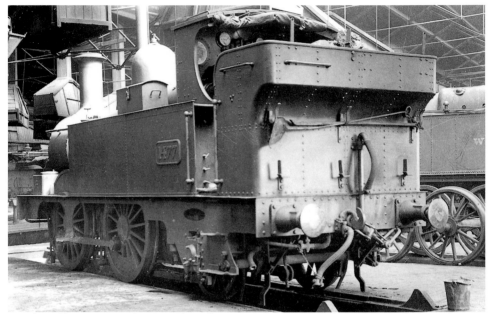

The Collett 0-4-2T was developed from the Armstrong '517' class. This example of the latter class is seen on Swindon Shed on 27th May, 1934.   *H.F. Wheeller Collection*

'5800' class 0-4-2T No. 5808, of the 1933 batch not having auto gear, sits nearly new at Swindon Shed.   *R.S. Carpenter Collection*

'Saint' class 4-6-0 No. 2935 *Caynham Court* which spent the latter part of its life modified with rotating cam poppet valve gear, the only such modification to be approved by Collett. *R.S. Carpenter/Lens of Sutton Collection*

One little research exercise which took place during all the work involving tank engines, was the modification in 1931 of 'Saint' class No. 2935 *Caynham Court* to try out rotary cam poppet valve gear. The locomotive was also fitted with new cylinders, but no marked benefit was found and this remained the only such conversion of this class and the only application of poppet valve gear on the GWR. The change also had added two tons to the weight. A number of modifications were made to the gear over the years of its installation which, in fact, lasted the life of the engine.

In keeping with other railways experimenting with pulverised coal as a fuel, the GWR involvement took place in late 1928, although at minimal cost to itself. In October of that year Collett received a request from William Beardmore & Co. for permission to equip a 'Saint' class 4-6-0 with its design of boiler and firebox capable of burning pulverised coal. All costs of the conversion would be covered by the firm. A locomotive was allocated and duly fitted out by Beardmore's, but the trials only lasted a brief time during 1929 before termination. Such fuel is incredibly dirty in use and facilities for its storage and discharge only existed in a very temporary form. It was, after all, not a Swindon idea and found little support from any of the Locomotive Department, particularly from the crews involved.

Although Stanier was in line to succeed Collett as CME, the age difference (he was now 56 to Collett's 61) meant that he might only serve a few years if Collett retired at 65. However, as we shall see shortly, Collett had plans to go on longer than that age and the opportunity came for him to let Stanier go in order that there would be no chance of a successor taking over until he felt need of retirement. Stanier was a very competent Assistant, perhaps posing a threat for Collett's retirement at a more normal 65. Although he and Collett appeared to be on friendly terms, it was thought by the few closely associated with them that there was some friction, particularly from Collett, but they had tended to dismiss this as part of the coming to terms with the loss of his wife.

Then, out of the blue came an offer to Stanier from the LMS, that of the position of CME, Sir Henry Fowler having moved into research at the beginning of 1931 and E.J. Lemon replacing him until a suitable successor was appointed.

0-6-0PT No. 5402 nears completion at Swindon in 1931.   *R.S. Carpenter Collection*

A class '5400' 0-6-0PT. This was a Collett version of the Armstrong '2021' class, a 55-year-old design by the time the update took place. No. 5416 is found at West Drayton on the Staines auto-train run in the late 1940s.   *John Scott-Morgan Collection*

This chance appeared to be an outlet which could benefit both Collett's and Stanier's ambitions and came at a time when a parting of the ways would be of inestimable value to the latter. Accordingly Stanier, encouraged by Collett, accepted the LMS post. Collett started looking round at his staff for a replacement, and selected someone never likely to pose a threat. This was John Auld, the former CME of the Barry Railway, who had been appointed Docks Assistant to him at Grouping. Auld was a few months older than Collett and proved to be a great asset, particularly in the latter years of Collett's tenure as CME, and could be relied upon absolutely, having built up a reputation for being friendly and approachable.

There is an interesting story associated with Stanier's departure, in that he had told Collett about the LMS approach immediately and suggested that the General Manager, Sir James Milne, be acquainted of the situation. Even though Milne was married to Stanier's sister-in-law, this formal notification was thought to be necessary, for Collett was a stickler for correctness and protocol. He therefore straight away arranged a meeting with Milne at Paddington and was in the process of informing him of the facts when the office door opened and in walked the Chairman, Viscount Churchill. Having picked up the gist of the conversation, Lord Churchill turned to Collett and said: 'Well, we want you to go your full course, and so there's no chance of Stanier becoming our CME'. For some time after this event, Collett inferred from this that the Chairman would like to see him in office until he was 70, for if Stanier had retired from the GWR normally at 65, he himself would be 70 at that time. In later years, if a hint as to the approach of his retirement was aired, he would pointedly refer to the fact that: 'The Chairman has asked me to stay in office until I am 70' - which he eventually did!

A range of tanks are undergoing repairs in Swindon 'B' shop on 30th August, 1931.
R.S. Carpenter Collection

Whilst Stanier was at Swindon, much of the liaison with the drawing office would have been his responsibility. He followed the Churchward precept of making sure he involved himself with those carrying out important tasks. Thus some measure of transmission of Collett's thoughts and desires was feasible. The drawing office staff, whilst glad of Stanier's friendly approach, had a degree of mistrust in Collett due to his remoteness. Had he bothered, even briefly, to lead them as a team, some respect would have grown and, as a result, a freer interchange of ideas occurred. This could have had the effect of not letting design stagnate. Stagnate it did, with the retention of low degree superheat and all 'new' locomotives really derivatives of Churchward's advanced concepts. It is clear that, quite often, the drawing office's thinking was transmitted by Stanier to Collett, but the latter resolutely refused to accept anything which did not fall into his rather narrow views on locomotive design matters. He was, after all, a production man and it was here that he was always to excel.

In 1932 Collett was once again elected as President of the ARLE, presiding at most meetings. The July meeting was notable for the presentation of a silver salver to Sir Henry Fowler on his relinquishing the post of Secretary to the Association after a long period.

The 19th December, 1933, was a black day for the ARLE, and the railway fraternity in general. Churchward, now retired nearly 12 years, and still living in the CME's residence at Swindon, was run down and killed by the down Fishguard express as it passed through Swindon. What possessed him to venture onto the track will never be known, but his hearing and eyesight were deteriorating and it has been speculated that he never heard the train until it was too late. At the first meeting of the ARLE following this tragedy the members stood in silence to mark their respect at the passing of this great engineer. This meeting was the last one at which Collett's attendance was recorded. He was beginning to withdraw from external bodies in his search for some means of coming to terms with his loss of Ethelwyn all those years ago.

Churchward, initially, had enjoyed a pleasant retirement, although the onset of myopia had affected his hobbies of horticulture (Newburn House had extensive gardens which he tended with the help of two gardeners), shooting, fishing and precision engineering. In the context of the last-mentioned he had, in the early years, carried out much of the maintenance work on his car. His early foray into the Grenville steam car had aroused a lifetime interest in vehicle modification and servicing. To this end he had a well-equipped workshop in the grounds of Newburn where he had been free to indulge in such work, his bachelor status permitting this as and when he liked.

Swindon came to a halt on 22nd December for the funeral of Churchward. Many of the workmen who had served during his time as CME were given the time off to attend and the mourners included Gresley, Stanier, Maunsell and, of course, Collett. Swindon Council was represented as were all the departments of the GWR.

It is of note that Collett's withdrawal from the ARLE came shortly after the death of Churchward. It was almost as if the death of the much respected retired CME caused a loss of behind-the-scenes support for continued membership, and brought about a loss of interest in this unofficial, yet very influential, body.

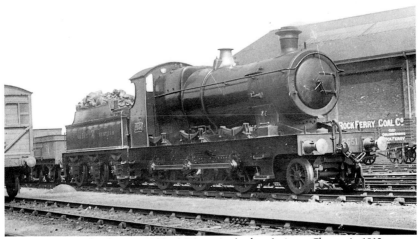

An immaculate 'Aberdare' 2-6-0 No. 2651 awaits further duties at Chester in 1912.
R.S. Carpenter Collection

Churchward had always been a forthcoming member, eager to share his ideas with those interested, whereas Collett's natural reticence to get heavily involved with other railways' ideas on design features was probably a further catalyst for his eventual withdrawal from the ARLE meetings. His spare time was to be increasingly filled with extraneous matters in the spiritual sphere.

Back in 1930 Collett had built a batch of Churchward's 2-8-0Ts, but as they were turned out the economic depression had struck and, combined with the increasing number of ships turning to oil-burning or diesel power, this reduced the demand for Welsh coal at the docks. The new tanks had been built to cover the transport of much of the coal no longer needed and were surplus to requirements, being stored from new. By 1933 it was apparent that these locomotives could be used to replace some of the old 'Aberdare' 2-6-0s, but their bunker capacity of 4 tons was inadequate for the longer runs. Collett ordered diagrams to be prepared for their conversion to 2-8-2T, the '7200' class, with extended rear frames and an enlarged bunker of 6 tons capacity. Some 54 were converted up to the outbreak of war out of the 205 examples in service. As a point of interest, the 2-8-0T had originally been schemed as a 2-8-2T, but was rejected as the wheelbase was thought to be too long for the Welsh valley lines on which they were to be used. The scheme for that 2-8-2T still rested in the archive drawers of the drawing office and so it was relatively simple, and inexpensive, to pull them out and update them for the rebuild.

The final offering to come from Collett in the form of a tank engine was the '1366' class 0-6-0PT for shunting work in yards where tight curvature was commonplace. This diminutive type, of which a batch of six was constructed, started their lives in Swindon wagon shops, as their short 11 ft wheelbase allowed

Another Churchward design retained by Collett was the '4200' class 2-8-0T, of which No. 5203 is found on an up mineral train on the Hereford to Worcester line in 1946-7.

John Scott-Morgan Collection

Drifting steam obscures the lines of 2-8-2T No. 7216, rebuilt from a 2-8-0T in 1934, at Swindon Shed on 28th February, 1937.   *R.S. Carpenter/H.F. Wheeller Collection*

them to go wherever a standard goods wagon could go. In later years they were to be found at Weymouth Docks and the former SR Wenford Bridge branch.

With Churchward now deceased, the CME's residence lay empty. Charles Collett showed no desire to live in it, although perfectly entitled to do so. He was, after all, a widower of some 10 years and, although Churchward had appeared happy to live a bachelor life in the substantial family house, had no desire to take it, and the staff employed, over. It sat in quite extensive grounds alongside the main line opposite the works and, with the need to provide space for a new carriage stock shed, this site was used. Sadly, the residence was pulled down to make way for the new shed, which sprawled across and obliterated the gardens which had been tended competently by three gardeners in Churchward's days. Collett approved this plan and it was as though he wished to eliminate a reminder of his predecessor, even though his own creations and expertise had a lot of Churchward in them and he himself owed so much of his experience to the great man.

As the troubled days of the depression passed, Swindon works was on short time, down to a three day week on occasion. In 1932 some 2,700 staff were laid off and 100 engines taken into storage due to reduced traffic. What irked Collett and his team was the fact that the Government was reducing unemployment in the North and Scotland by ordering the transfer of work to there from Swindon. This only aggravated the unemployment situation in and around Swindon.

However, some of the job losses were due to Collett's continuation of the Churchward standardisation policy combined with the continued drive for precision manufacture, both of which combined to give more miles between shoppings and, consequently, required less manpower for the reduced maintenance tasks.

The '1366' class consisted of just six engines, they were unusual by GWR standards in being outside-cylindered pannier tanks. They had a wheelbase of just 11 ft, the wheelbase of a '57XX' class pannier tank was 15 ft 6 in. This view shows the first of the class, No. 1366.

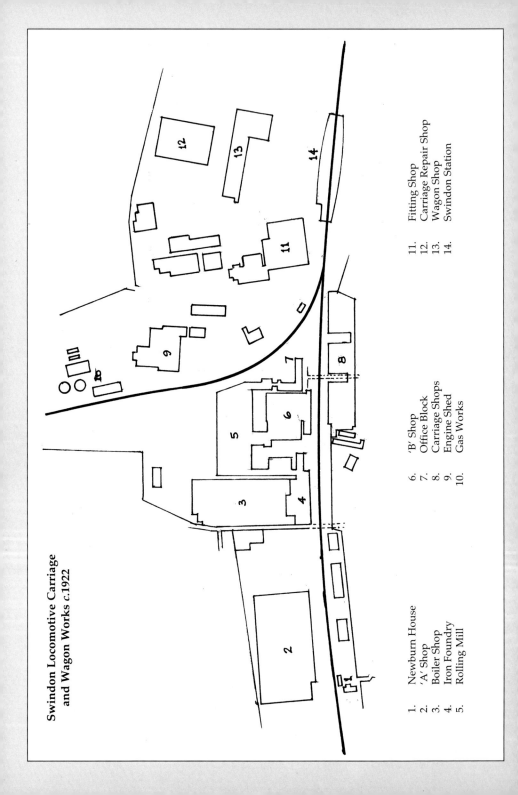

**Swindon Locomotive Carriage
and Wagon Works c.1922**

1. Newburn House
2. 'A' Shop
3. Boiler Shop
4. Iron Foundry
5. Rolling Mill

6. 'B' Shop
7. Office Block
8. Carriage Shops
9. Engine Shed
10. Gas Works

11. Fitting Shop
12. Carriage Repair Shop
13. Wagon Shop
14. Swindon Station

Chapter Nine

Works Improvements and Carriage and Wagon Stock Developments

One small, but important, responsibility of the CME at Swindon was that of the maintenance and up-dating of locomotive depots over the system. In 1916, at the redefining of the Locomotive Superintendent's responsibilities to that of Chief Mechanical Engineer, one of the matters remaining under the CME was that of locomotive depots and works throughout the GWR. In 1926, Collett's first major decision in such matters was the remodelling of the ex-Rhymney Railway works at Caerphilly. This permitted the major servicing of GWR locomotives in South Wales at one site. Some 60 engines could be accommodated in the rebuilt works. The extra personnel needed were drawn from many of the other locomotive works in that area following their run-down and closure.

So far as locomotive sheds were concerned, the first big developments under Collett were those at Llanelly in 1925 and Stourbridge in 1926. Both these were of the standard Churchward units built around turntables. Following this, a series of some nine straight road sheds were also planned and built between 1929 and 1934, some including a separate repair shop. The provisions of the 1929 Loans and Guarantees Act were taken as an opportunity to achieve this, by now sorely needed, update in facilities.

In 1932, to help take pressure off Swindon works, the Stafford Road works at Wolverhampton was extensively rebuilt. It was then capable of dealing with the heaviest engines for major overhaul, but no production was recommenced there.

One little quirk of Collett's, associated with his immediate staff, was the fact that, whilst encouraging them to obtain membership of the Institutions of both Civil and Mechanical Engineers, he made it quite plain that he would not allow them to consider joining the Institution of Locomotive Engineers. He was of the opinion that this latter organisation was little more than a forum for 'commercial travellers', as a large number of members were from the private locomotive builders. It was as though his thinking was influenced by a strict partisanship with regard to locomotive design and construction carried out by the railways themselves, these in his opinion, being superior to the products of private industry. This despite the fact that he, himself, had used their services a short time previously in the case of Armstrong Whitworth, Bagnall, Beyer, Peacock, North British, Kerr, Stuart and the Yorkshire Engine Co., although this was under pressure from the Board to take advantage of the Government's aid package to place work in depressed areas. It was as well that he did not succeed in impressing some of his immediate staff to follow his own thoughts absolutely, for when Stanier moved to the LMS he used the private builders extensively in his 'scrap and build' programme on that railway.

On the GWR, as on the Southern Railway, the CME was responsible for carriage and wagon stock developments. The other railways preferred to provide Carriage and Wagon Engineers to relieve the CME of the considerable responsibilities in this area.

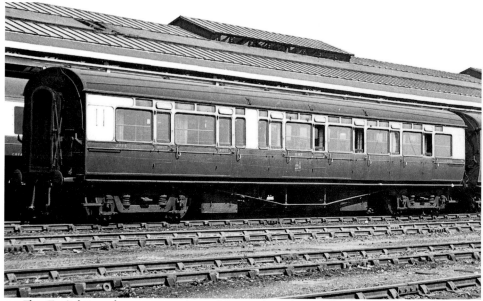

The 'Toplight' coaches were popular and in use throughout Collett's days. This first/third example of such stock is seen at Tyseley.   *R.S. Carpenter/P.J. Garland Collection*

Introduced by Churchward in 1904, the 70 ft 'Dreadnought' stock had distinctive inset doors. This example, a brake third was photographed in Tyseley carriage sidings on 25th May, 1948.   *R.S. Carpenter/P.J. Garland Collection*

The standard bogie employed for all principal express stock was based on the Dean 9 ft wheelbase item, and with riding qualities being one of Collett's interests, he soon had the carriage section of the drawing office spend much time on modernising this unit. Many improvements had been made over the years to this bogie and Collett introduced improved methods of frame construction, utilising pressed plates which were manufactured on the large press in the boiler shop. However, when used in connection with the 70 ft bodies used for major expresses these bogies did suffer a greater rate of flange wear than on other, shorter, vehicles. The attendant maintenance costs were becoming worrying, so Collett, shortly after taking office as CME, ordered that all new standard stock should be designed to the more normal 57 ft length. A 7 ft wheelbase bogie was also standardised for stock used on suburban and semi-fast trains.

A further change to carriage stock made at this time, mentioned in Chapter Four, was the reversion to the old GWR chocolate and cream livery from the maroon then standard. This livery was, as the years advanced, to become much simpler in its application of complex lining as the structure of the bodies became smoother with the more modern styling and construction techniques.

So far as design changes were concerned, in 1923, Collett agreed to the trials of buckeye couplings and Pullman type gangways. The latter of these fittings never became standard on the GWR, as fully to implement them would mean refitting all existing stock if complete interchangeability between sets and individual strengthening coaches was to be retained. Buckeye couplings, however, were placed on new stock with additional special drop-down buffers provided to permit connection to coaches having normal screw couplings. Raising these into position permitted mixing of new and old stock.

Articulation of coaches was tried and some of the 1925-built stock comprised two- or three-car articulated sets. Examples of these were displayed on the GWR express train sent to Darlington for the centenary celebrations there that year. Some suburban sets, used around London, also employed articulation at this time. These latter sets continued in use into the 1950s, but the express variants were rebuilt as conventional bogie coaches in the late 1930s.

Coach production in the 1920s was, initially, on the increase, from 210 in 1924 to 295 in 1927, to replace old out-of-date stock. Additionally, the carriage works was expected to overhaul some 4,000 vehicles every year. Charles Collett kept himself fully aware of the needs in this area and ordered that new designs be prepared for consideration as the 1930s approached. Even a small number of new slip coaches, a GWR speciality, were ordered. These were improved to allow slipping at high speed, with a redesigned uncoupling system to permit this.

A smooth ride was, to Collett, indicative of good bogie design and, after taking office as CME he decided to investigate the riding qualities of the seven main types of bogie then in service. He ordered that a test train of seven coaches be made up, with each coach having a different kind of bogie. In order to get an idea as to the riding quality, the lavatory tanks in each coach were filled with a whitewash mix of a different colour. Observers in the lavatory compartments were ordered to release some wash whenever a bad lurch was felt. Examination

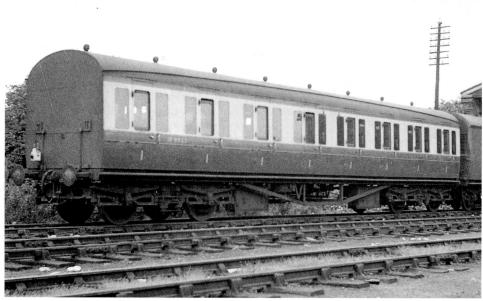

A non-corridor first, built in 1937 to Diagram A21.   *Joe Moss Collection*

A standard 57 ft 8-compartment third as built during Collett's days. It is photographed here at Birmingham (Snow Hill) on 11th October, 1947.   *R.S. Carpenter/P.J. Garland Collection*

of the resulting colour of the ballast then gave an indication of the bogies' reaction to track defects. If all the colours appeared at one point, clearly the track was at fault. By this very basic, but effective, approach the best-riding bogies were determined for future standardisation.

As the other railways made extensive use of Pullman cars, the Board asked for their consideration for, in particular, the prestigious Ocean Liner specials to and from Plymouth. A set was purloined, sufficient for this train, in 1929 and entered service offering the passengers a large degree of comfort and service. They were also used on the short-lived 'Torquay Pullman'. Collett felt that it would be more economic if the GWR built its own luxury stock. And so, in 1931 eight 'Super Saloons' were constructed. These were every bit as comfortable and plush as the discarded Pullmans and took advantage of the generous GWR loading gauge to adopt a width of 9 ft 7 in. The interiors were modelled on those of the Pullmans and this set was used through to the war years on all liner specials and prestige expresses to the West Country.

Around 1930, as excursion trains were becoming ever more popular, the carriage and wagon drawing section of the drawing office prepared some diagrams for centre-corridor coaches. These had tables between facing pairs of seats and were very similar in layout to stock on the other railways which had been in service for a few years. They proved very popular and were frequently used for strengthening the summer expresses to the West Country resorts.

Further developments of the restyled express stock appeared in 1935. These were known as the 'Centenary' coaches, as 100 years previously the GWR had been established. Two complete trains of this new stock, with a width of 9 ft 7 in., were built in 1935 for the 'Cornish Riviera Limited'. Comprising 10 vehicles plus a three-car kitchen and dining set they incorporated some very high-class interiors for this, the principal express of the GWR. They went into service on the 8th July, 1935. These carriages were notable for the elimination of a separate door to each compartment, entry being by end vestibules only. The compartments now had picture windows, which gave the passengers a much improved view.

That mundane, but vitally important item, the wagon, was yet to be much updated, so most of the less important freight trains were still comprised of unbraked vehicles in the main. However, despite this, the GWR was one of the foremost employers of braked goods stock. Most of the specialised vehicles such as closed vans, milk vans, utility vans, cattle wagons, horse boxes and milk tanker wagons were vacuum braked in order that they could be marshalled into passenger trains as well as being used on express freight services. In fact, some 12 of the latter services departed from Paddington Goods station each night. Many of these trains, which were limited to a speed of 60 mph, employed the 'Hall' class mixed traffic types, which remained in production throughout the 1930s. The milk tank wagons were a new development of the 1930s, and with their glass-lined tanks of 3,000 gallons capacity mounted on 6-wheel undercarriages weighed 28 tons loaded. So a train of some 12 of these vehicles would weigh about the same as a typical express and, bearing in mind that the daily requirement of milk for London was 240,000 gallons, some seven or eight trainloads would just about cover this. The bigger mixed-traffic locomotives

In 1933 a batch of three mail vans, complete with pick-up gear was built for the London to West of England services. They were 50 ft long and were to Diagram L22.

R.S. Carpenter/P.J. Garland Collection

The ubiquitous 'B' set, used on many branch lines of the GWR.

R.S. Carpenter/P.J. Garland Collection

Some of the 'Centenary' stock were built as sleeping cars. Here No. W9080 has at some time been fitted with 6-wheel bogies. Tyseley Carriage sidings, April 1950.

R.S. Carpenter/P.J. Garland Collection

Frequently large bogie vans would be marshalled in passenger trains. Here a Siphon G, often used for perishable goods, is so found. *R.S. Carpenter/P.J. Garland Collection*

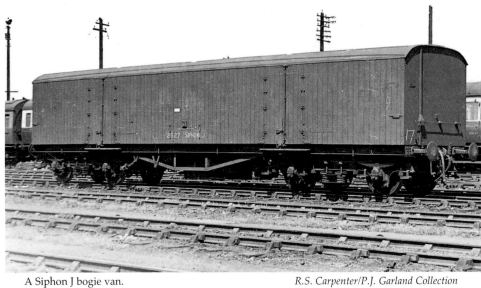

A Siphon J bogie van.   *R.S. Carpenter/P.J. Garland Collection*

A long wheelbase parcels van.   *R.S. Carpenter/P.J. Garland Collection*

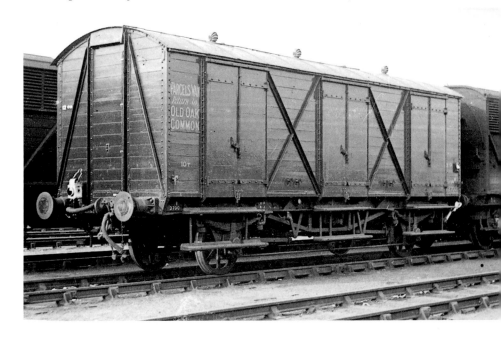

came into their own on such workings at night, often being rostered for some passenger work during the day.

With the large 2-8-0s capable of hauling in excess of 100 wagons special driving skills were called for to prevent division during braking or starting manoeuvres on the heavy coal trains from Wales. Despite advances in freight stock that dreadful British legacy, the unbraked freight, was still very much alive on the GWR (and other railways) in Collett's days.

Although private owner wagons still proliferated, the Great Western still built, for its own use, some 2,000 vehicles each year. With the repair throughput of some 15,000 vehicles every year the wagon shops were most certainly busy. These shops also built bodies for the company's motor vehicles as well as standard containers which could be transferred from lorries onto flat trucks for transit throughout the system.

Sir Felix Pole, the General Manager from 1921, had taken a close look at the extensive coal traffic which employed thousands of these private owner wagons, mostly of 10-12 tons capacity. He suggested that considerable economies could be had by employing 20 ton steel wagons and proposed their design and introduction. Such vehicles would save on siding space, a figure of 35 per cent reduction being estimated, and also on maintenance costs due to the stronger steel bodies. The collieries in South Wales were reluctant to invest in any changes to their facilities to accommodate the longer wagons, even though Pole offered a reduction of 5 per cent in carriage charges. The GWR went ahead however, with 1,000 wagons being ordered in 1924, the first of which entered traffic on the 27th August of that year, following the approval of the designs. They proved popular and within a year 11 companies were using them, with some collieries embarking on a replacement of their privately owned vehicles with this design.

However, the 1926 coal strike crippled the mines financially, so there was no chance of any further investment to allow a complete change to these larger wagons and the old private owner vehicles soldiered on through to Nationalisation. This attempt at modernisation failed due to events outside the control of the GWR.

Specialised wagon developments on the GWR were an important part of the CME's responsibilities. Although the 20 ton mineral wagon episode was thwarted by circumstances outside the railway's control, there were several more instances where developments were implemented to improve the railway's ability to offer efficient freight transport.

Throughout the 1930s the GWR freight stock averaged around 80,000 vehicles of all kinds. Developments in this decade started with the 'Mink G', a 20 ton high capacity van which was designed for use in fitted freights. The wheelbase was a few inches under 20 feet and vacuum braking standard, the 'Instanter' coupling being fitted. Just prior to the introduction of these vans, a batch of 30 ton vans had been introduced.

Some specialised containers to be used on the flat wagons were developed as the GWR road transport system was progressively enlarged and improved. Some of these were designed for the transport of bicycles and others for perishable goods were fitted with the 'Drikold' solid carbon dioxide refigeration system, a development of the ICI plant at Billingham.

Two of the 20 ton steel coal wagons introduced in the 1920s. No. 0326 (nearest) has end doors whilst the other (53428) is specifically for loco coal.   *R.S. Carpenter Collection*

The container flat wagon was used extensively by the GWR for loads which required transferring to road transport.   *John Scott-Morgan Collection*

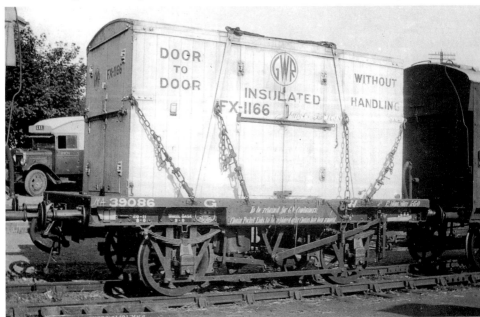

This fruit van was built in 1938 for the fitted freight services. Note the 'Not common user' and 'Return to Weymouth Quay' inscriptions. *R.S. Carpenter Collection*

A rather grubby 6-wheel milk tanker caught at Birmingham (Snow Hill) in 1947. *R.S. Carpenter/P.J. Garland Collection*

The earlier four- and six-wheeled milk tankers were supplemented by demountable units carried on flat trucks, again aimed at the enhanced road transport system. The considerable seasonal traffic in fruit and vegetables resulted in some 200 'Fruit As' 12 ton ventilated and vacuum braked vans being introduced in 1938. Earlier, in 1935, the 'Grano' 20 ton hopper wagon for grain had been turned out, again vacuum fitted.

Some very specialised six-wheeled insulated vans for the transport of Palethorpes 'Royal Cambridge' sausages had been provided, to keep the substantial contract for the transport of this product from the clutches of the competitive road transport system.

The C&W section of the drawing office was kept busy planning all the new vehicles and Collett added the overseeing of their design as part of his extensive responsibilities. Stanier had gone, but the team of Auld, Hawksworth, Cook and their staffs coped efficiently with the demands placed on their respective skills as their CME, at times, settled back into quiet contemplation of more extraneous matters.

The standard GWR 'Toad' 16 ton brake van. This example is found at Malmesbury in 1949. Note the unusual tied concrete block sleepers.   *Joe Moss Collection*

Chapter Ten

Railcars, Streamlining and Production Techniques

Before launching into the railcar story, a short aside in connection with another member of the Collett family on the GWR is appropriate.

Although he had little direct connection with the CME's department, the GWR Assistant Secretary, Stanley Beresford Collett was descended from the head of the Gloucestershire Colletts, Thomas, and the connection to Charles can be traced back at 12 generations.

S.B. Collett was the third child of Sir Charles Henry Collett, Bart, and had served in the RFC as a pilot during World War I. He flew DH4s in 50 Squadron and was engaged on pioneering long range bombing raids on Germany, eventually being awarded the Croix de Guerre. At the end of the war he was a Squadron Leader.

After the war Stanley qualified as a solicitor and joined the GWR in that capacity. One of his first tasks was to study rail and air co-operation, for in the late 1920s the idea of being involved in air transport germinated with the Boards of the four main lines, with Sir Felix Pole of the GWR being one of the leading protagonists. His influence on the other main railways resulted in a Parliamentary Bill in 1929 giving them provisions under which they might operate air services. Royal Assent was given to this Bill on 10th May, 1929 and the railways then had powers to operate air services within their own territories and in Europe as far as 20°E (that is nearly as far as Warsaw or Belgrade). Under the Bill they were forbidden to manufacture aeroplanes or aero engines.

The initial findings of the discussions amongst the railways were that, as no regular internal air services existed, there appeared to be no call to set up any permanent operation just then. However, by 1933 some internal air routes became a reality and the GWR, in March of that year, held talks with Imperial Airways to discuss the proposal that it begin using its 1929 powers. The route initially agreed was between Cardiff and Plymouth via Haldon, where GWR buses connected to Newton Abbot, Torquay and Teignmouth. Imperial Airways was to provide the aircraft, crew and engineers with the GWR supplying traffic staff. The total trip time, including bus transfers at each end, was some three hours less than that achievable on the route via the Severn Tunnel.

A three-engined Westland Wessex machine, carrying six passengers, suitably registered G-AAGW and painted in chocolate and cream, was chartered from Imperial Airways and the service inaugurated on 11th April, 1933. The passenger list for that first flight of this pioneering service was:

Mr Geoffrey F. Luttrell - a GWR Director
Mr A. Maynard - Chief Goods Manager, GWR
Mr S.B. Collett - Assistant Secretary, GWR
Mr A.S. Quartermaine - Assistant Chief Civil Engineer, GWR
Mr F.C.A. Coventry - Superintendent of Road Transport, GWR
and a representative of the *Western Mail*

A Westland Wessex, G-AAGW, the aircraft which inaugurated the GWR air service in 1933. A manufacturer's photograph of it in experimental guise to test the alternative in-line engines to the standard radials.   *Royal Aeronautical Society Collection*

By 1936, the mainstay of many RAS routes was the four-engined de Havilland DH86. Here G-ACVY *Mercury* of that fleet delivers mails at one of the destinations. This aircraft was issued with its Certificate of Airworthiness on 15th August, 1934 and delivered soon after. It survived the War as a communications aircraft and was eventually retired and broken up in 1948.

Royal Aeronautical Society Collection

The pioneering internal air service set up by the GWR was unique in one particular sense. It provided the first regular Air Mail service in the UK. The conveyance of mail in the UK was the monopoly of the Postmaster General, but there was a special concession made to the railway companies in that they were permitted to convey letters not exceeding 2 oz. weight for an additional fee of 3*d*. These were categorised as 'Railway Letters'. This concession had been interpreted as being applicable to all services, rail, road and, ultimately, air, in which the GWR had a controlling interest and, therefore, from the inaugural air service, mails were carried on all regular flights.

The first operations, until the Railway Air Services (RAS) appeared as a co-operative venture in 1934, only carried a little over 700 passengers and 4 cwt of mail. The GWR lost £6,500 in that time but the venture helped lay the foundations for a feasible internal air service, for in January 1934 Railway Air Services Ltd was formed and ratified by all Boards concerned. This company was registered on 21st March, 1934, the Directors being:

Sir Harold Hartley (LMS)
S.B. Collett (GWR)
O.H. Corble (LNER)
G.S. Szlumper (SR)
Lt-Col H. Burchell (Imperial Airways)

This company was to inaugurate many internal air services over the years up to World War II with a growing fleet of mainly de Havilland types.

The reconstituted RAS eventually had an extensive network of services and laid the ground for a comprehensive air mail service throughout the UK, the concept having been proved by the 1933 GWR initiative.

Charles Collett's thoughts and comments on this venture into the aviation sphere are not on record, but as his Department had no input into the operation, the scheme probably generated little interest, as around this time other technological advances were appearing on the horizon in the form of diesel railcars.

Sadly, Stanley Collett was killed a few weeks after his RAS Board appointment whilst flying as a crew member of No. 600 Squadron of the RAF Reserve, which he had led in previous years. A flight of their planes was participating in the 1934 Hendon Air Pageant and the machine he was crewing had, it appears, engine failure occasioned by fuel starvation. The pilot steered it away from the crowd, only to side-slip into the ground and burst into flames.

For many years now the GWR had employed steam railmotors on lightly used branch line and cross-country services. Churchward had started the trend in 1903 by introducing two such vehicles following trials carried out using a Drummond railmotor borrowed from the LSWR. Such was the usefulness of these inexpensive and economic vehicles that, by 1908, a total of 99 was in service over the network of branches. Unfortunately, the habit of attaching extra vehicles led to the wearing out of these low powered units and frequent repairs were called for. There was also the limitation on train times set by the top speed of 40 mph of these otherwise successful units, for they were far and above the best of all the many railmotors built by the railways in the first decade of the century. Also, the need to remove the motor bogie for repairs in the locomotive works, whilst sending the body to the

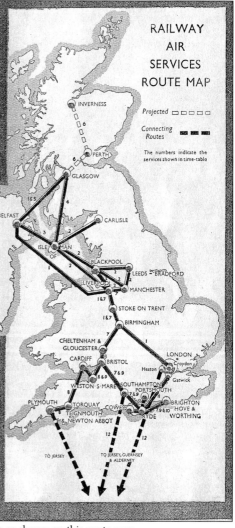

By 1936 the Railway Air Services were expanding as shown on this route map.

Royal Aeronautical Society Library

This photograph shows the power unit of a GWR steam railmotor at Swindon in 1932.

R.S. Carpenter Collection

Steam railmotor No. 62 on a Paddington working at Denham in 1908.

R.S. Carpenter Collection

The first railcar design had only rudimentary buffing gear and was fully shrouded over the bogies. A vehicle clearly ahead of its time. No. 2 caught at Tyseley in 1936.

R.S. Carpenter Collection

The second batch of railcars followed the first in general design and were operated as single units. No. W8 at Birmingham (Snow Hill) *c.*1956.   *R.S. Carpenter Collection*

carriage works for attention, tended to increase the overall time out of service for repairs. From 1915 onwards a programme of conversion of the railmotors to auto-train trailers was instigated, but some survived unchanged until the early 1930s, when Collett took stock of the need to replace them and find some means of eliminating the auto-train system. This, being locomotive powered, was now being affected by the rising cost of coal which threatened to swallow up the limited returns from this sparsely used, but essential, traffic. During a study of current developments in the railway sphere, the German diesel train technology then being developed came to notice, for it was around this time that the 'Flying Hamburger' was being developed to provide a streamlined high-speed luxury express service. This new development was receiving a great deal of publicity in railway circles. Collett accordingly asked for funds to purchase a trial diesel unit for some evaluation. These were granted and a contract placed with the Associated Equipment Company of Southall for a single example.

In December 1933 this prototype was delivered, and in styling and concept was to form a watershed in branch line and main line work covering services which could be satisfied more economically by this new form of vehicle. It was powered by a single 121 bhp AEC/Ricardo diesel engine mounted under the floor, and had a most up-to-date streamlined body with seating for a maximum of 69 passengers. The driver had a cab at each end of the body and the maximum speed was 60 mph. This prototype was put into service for a press publicity run from Paddington to Reading, on 1st December, 1933. The 36 mile journey was covered in 40 minutes. Bearing in mind that this vehicle was only capable of 60 mph, it was a creditable performance. The quoted price of £3,000 was competitive enough for further orders to be considered early the following year, Collett's original worry about first cost being allayed by this figure. This unit was placed in service at Reading and proved most popular and efficient, even though it was somewhat under-powered. This resulted in a further three being ordered in 1934 for express passenger services. These had twin 121 bhp engines, a buffet car section and two lavatories, and seated 44 passengers for whom a luggage compartment was provided. These modifications raised the price to £3,500, which was still acceptable to Collett. They were capable of 80 mph and placed the GWR at the forefront of passenger diesel rail developments in the UK. One of the cross-country routes on which these faster cars was employed was the 105 mile Birmingham to Cardiff run.

By the end of 1934 the clear potential of the diesel railcar was there for all to see and a further 13 vehicles were authorised, this time from the Gloucester Railway Carriage and Wagon Co., using the same AEC/Ricardo twin engines as the earlier models, the first of which entered service in July 1935.

The economy and immediacy of these railcars led to further developments in 1937 for a Swindon-built version, No. 18, with one important difference, this being the ability to haul a tail load of up to 60 tons. For this the new variant was fitted with standard buffers and drawgear and hose couplings, and, more importantly, controls to permit it to be driven from a driving trailer. Despite his steam background, Collett was fully aware of advantages conferred by using other means of motive power. More developments were to come as the 1930s progressed with a follow-on batch of 20 units proposed, four of which were to be formed into two-car units with potential for fitting a trailer car between

The success of the railcars led to the development of a purely express parcels version, of which two were built. No. 17 at Sonning *c.*1947.   *John Scott-Morgan Collection*

Trials with No. 18 proved the capability of the unit to have an additional coach - in this case an auto-trailer - attached for extra capacity. On trial on the Brentford branch before entering service in 1937.   *R.S. Carpenter Collection*

The final batches of railcars had a much more angular appearance. No. 23 seen at Bristol (Temple Meads), *c.*1949.   *R.S. Carpenter/Joe Moss Collection*

The last series of railcars were designed to be operated in pairs, often with a trailer coach marshalled in between. The precursor of the BR dmu set. Here Nos. 35 and 36 leave Bristol (Temple Meads) in 1955.   *R.S. Carpenter Collection*

'King' class No. 6014 *King Henry VII* in 'A' shop Swindon in March 1935, for modification to the semi-streamlined shape devised by Collett. *R.S. Carpenter Collection*

'Castle' class 4-6-0 No. 5005 *Manorbier Castle* with the full streamlining, including the tender shroud, at Old Oak Common. A rare shot, as it was not long before bits began to be removed *R.S. Carpenter Collection*

them, making them the forerunner of what was to become the dmu in the future under the nationalised BR.

These dmu sets were not, in fact, to materialise until Charles Collett had retired, as they used power-units common to military heavy-duty vehicles. The approach of World War II meant that priority had to be given to the military use and it was not until 1941 that they could be provided for the railway.

So far as other internal combustion powered vehicles were concerned on the GWR, there was a single 350 hp 0-6-0 diesel-electric shunter delivered in 1937 for use in the Acton yard, plus six Simplex petrol-engined shunters for use at various locations and, at Swindon, two 70 hp 0-4-0 Fowler diesel-mechanical shunters which spent their lives in and around the wagon shops.

As this development work moved forward, Charles Collett relinquished the JP status he had held now for 17 years. He needed more of his spare time to be available for what was fast becoming an obsession, the study of metaphysics and psychical research. He was beginning to withdraw more and more to himself, such that only those of a long association with him could get through on design matters. He also preferred the more mundane matters arising from the staff as the current designs progressed to be dealt with by his Assistants.

The ARLE was less on his agenda from this time onwards, the contact with this body, so far as the GWR was concerned, continued through Hawksworth being delegated to attend the meetings and maintain the link with design matters and standardisation policies discussed.

Hawksworth, now a Principal Assistant, was clearly in favour of some radical changes in design matters, still firmly grounded in those determined in the opening years of the century. He realised the benefits of better superheating and higher boiler pressures, but Collett could not be persuaded to depart from that which, to him, seemed perfectly adequate for his steam locomotives. On the other hand, he most certainly appeared to wish to pursue the diesel railcar development. So, at least in the railcar scene, the GWR was ahead of the rest of the British railways.

Before the new railcars were designed and tested, the diesel developments in Germany mentioned earlier, which employed streamlining as an aid to achieving the high speeds used in service, coupled with some developments in the USA, sparked off an application of streamlining to some of the latest British locomotive developments. Collett on the GWR responded by ordering the drawing office to prepare some diagrams based on his own application of plasticine to a model of the 'Castle' class. The result was a peculiar mix of shapes, the most prominent being a huge hemispherical projection on the smokebox. Little benefit could be gained from these changes, indeed the fairing over the cylinders led directly to some overheating in that area. Gradually, the offending shapes were removed from the two locomotives chosen as guinea-pigs, *King Henry VII* and *Manorbier Castle*, and the experiment quietly died. The employment of streamlining, other than the railcars, never had any other application at Swindon to the end of its days. And even the latter series of railcars designed and built at Swindon were, in the interests of production cost, much more angular in shape and could only loosely be classed as streamlined. Gresley, on the LNER, was next in the streamlined locomotive scene with his classic 'A4' Pacific, closely followed by Stanier on the LMS. The Southern remained aloof from it until Bulleid took office.

After initial trials of the 'streamlined' King had shown some effects of overheating of cylinders and difficulty of access to the rocking shafts of the motion, the final modification looked like this until quietly removed a short time after introduction. 'The Torbay Express' in 1935. *John Scott-Morgan Collection*

In fact Collett on the GWR had been the first to apply streamlining principles to British steam locomotives, and one wonders what might have happened if the exercise had been taken a bit more seriously. Swindon would have led the way in that field as well as in diesel railcars.

However lax in design advances as was obvious in the streamlining episode, Swindon was not backward so far as testing techniques go, for there was one piece of equipment in its hands which was unique. This was the stationary locomotive test plant built under Churchward in 1905. This permitted the testing, under controlled circumstances, of locomotives. As originally designed this plant could only absorb about 500 horse power, which restricted its potential somewhat. Some limited use of it was made by Collett, who quickly realised the limits placed by the restricted power absorption. He accordingly started quietly planning for an upgrade to this facility in the early 1930s. At this time, Gresley was proposing a national locomotive testing station, similar to that at Vitre-sur-Seine in France, to which he was planning on sending his new express 2-8-2 for some trials. Stanier, on the LMS, was in general agreement and an approach was made to the GWR to see if they would care to be involved and share the cost of setting up a plant.

However, Collett, although scarcely involved in affairs external to the GWR, did make sure that he kept himself aware of moves elsewhere in railway and engineering technology. He ensured that he read all relevant technical reports and that these were constantly brought to his attention. In this way he kept himself informed of all that was going on and, therefore, his response to the test plant suggestion mentioned above was an invitation to the LNER and LMS CME departments to visit him at Swindon. Upon their arrival, the representatives sent were taken along to 'A' shop to find, to their astonishment, a completely re-furbished and up-graded plant absorbing the full output of No. 2931 *Arlington Court* at 70 mph! Collett had produced, for the GWR, what was to remain a pipe-dream for many years on the other railways. Not even 'old boy' Stanier had realised that the changes had been made. Swindon independence still asserted itself.

One further example of awareness in new technology, so far as Collett was concerned, stemmed from his being a proponent of manufacturing accuracy.

The staff were encouraged to peruse the technical press for new developments to aid the improvement of tolerances. One particular item which often involved many man-hours was that of setting up the alignment of frames such that the horn faces were within a specified tolerance, plus ensuring that the cylinder to driving axle distances were as specified. Sometimes this involved a total length of 20 ft being covered.

Collett realised that large tolerances involved slack fits and consequent heavy wear and, more importantly, noise. Tighter tolerances would reduce such effects. As regards the noise aspect, a locomotive producing any form of excessive noise from connecting or coupling rods was expected to be reported by any member of the technical staff in order that its shed might be contacted for an explanation.

Around 1931-32 some developments in Germany by Carl Zeiss of an optical method for locomotive frame alignment was noted. Upon receiving notification of this Collett obtained authority to purchase a set of this equipment, his interest in precision manufacture still being very much in his mind. Zeiss accepted the GWR order and, once delivered and the fitters trained to use it, this became a standard feature of the Swindon production line. The first locomotives to benefit from its use were the last of the 1934 batch of 'Castles', Nos. 5023 to 5032, which resulted in Intermediate Repair mileages of 120,000 becoming more or less standard, with General Repair mileages reaching 400,000. Subsequent to this batch a further 10 were built in 1935, Nos. 5033-5042, which had the reputation of being the best batch ever built. Their running was smoother and high speeds more easily attained when compared with the earlier examples built to the old standards. This improvement was indeed to reduce the overall maintenance costs by a significant amount on all locomotives assembled in this way.

One notable feature under Collett was the changes in locomotive stock, mileages and fuel consumption between, for example, 1927 and 1937. The following table shows the improvements wrought over that decade due to, largely, better maintenance and production techniques:

Year	Locos in Stock	Mileages	Miles per loco	Available for duty	
1927	4,088	95,953,179	23,172	74.6%	
1937	3,621	100,421,983	27,718	82.0%(min)	90.0%(max)
% change	-11.0	+4.7	+18.0	+7.4 to +15.4	

The above statistics speak volumes for Charles Collett's handling of the manufacture and servicing of the GWR fleet. With rising coal costs as the end of the above decade approached, the coal consumption reduction of approximately 4¾ per cent, which went with the above data, was particularly useful in the never-ending fight to hold costs down in a grossly under-funded situation.

An indication as to how seriously Collett took the works' manning situation is best lillustrated by this quote from Sir Hugh Ford, one time Premium Apprentice at Swindon from 1927:

My only other experience (of C.B. Collett) was in my first weeks at Swindon. For the first month a new apprentice worked with an experienced fitter to learn the ropes. Mr Rice

The Optical frame alignment equipment layout

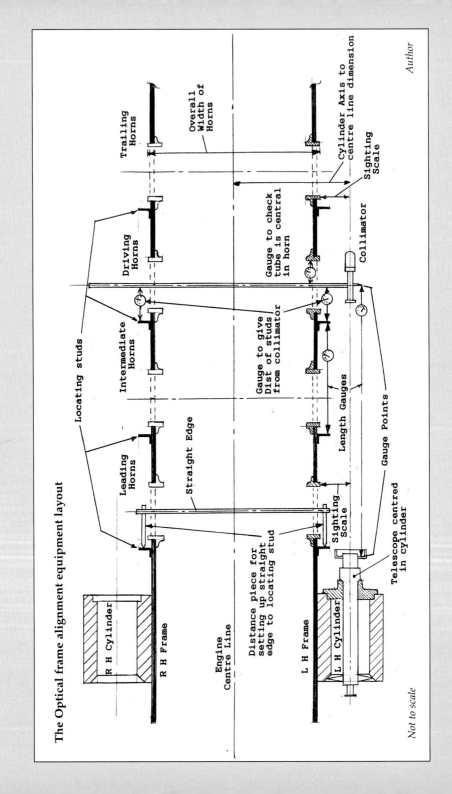

Not to scale

Author

(the fitter) had been sent out into the sidings to fit an 0-6-0 tank engine with an automatic train control shoe and naturally I had to go out with him. The message came down to the shop foreman that to do that job was a 'one-man job', with instructions to withdraw the second hand! Presumably the circumstance was explained, since we heard no more about it.

Clearly, although not involving himself directly in the manning issues, Collett's keen eyes had noticed that two hands were engaged in a task which should normally be covered by one fitter, and had promptly sent an appropriate message to the relevant foreman.

To revert to the earlier paragraphs of this chapter, the steam auto-train was to remain a GWR institution, even into BR days. Had the war not come along in 1939, probably further expansion of diesel units would have been possible, thus displacing the steam units completely on the grounds of single-manning and economic operating costs. Intransingent Collett may have been on his steam designs, but he certainly placed the GWR at the forefront in the application of diesel power for passenger services in the UK. The other main railways were content to restrict diesel to shunting operations thus far.

It does seem peculiar that, whilst so far ahead with diesel-powered passenger units, Collett ignored the clear potential the diesel engine had in the shunting area. The other railways, notably the LMS and Southern, were introducing diesel-mechanical or diesel-electric shunting locomotives which were proving very versatile and able machines. Their capabilities of being in use 24 hours a day with minimal servicing gave considerable economies of operation. Charles Collett, however, appeared to ignore such possibilities. But, of course, the GWR was still struggling to maintain a satisfactory operating profit, only really achieving one which precluded any major investment in new technology.

In other areas concerned with constructional techniques, Collett was not behind developments elsewhere. The GWR had stayed with the use of copper for firebox construction throughout his time as CME, despite other railways experimenting with steel fireboxes. The old trusted method of assembly using lapped, riveted joints had been used for almost a century now and he wished to consider changing this to an all-welded assembly. The news that some experimental work with copper welding was being carried out in Europe came to his notice. He called in Hannington, the Works Manager, and delegated him to organise some visits to France and Germany to find out what he could about this new welding technology. Hannington departed on this trip, taking with him the boilermaker welding foreman, H. Eburne.

The outcome of this visit to the Continent was to confirm the feasibility of welding copper in a production environment and Collett ordered that Swindon should develop its own techniques based on what had been gleaned over there. The result of the development programme was a success and firebox welding became standard practice in the works, with seams as long as 9 ft being dealt with on a regular basis. This was to be at the forefront of copper welding practice in the UK. The process soon became a showpiece in the works and was eventually to prove most helpful in advancing boiler maintenance and thereby reducing the Running Department's costs.

The original 'Duke' class was quite an elegant design, here No. 3276 *Dartmoor* is in ex-works condition at Oxford in 1904.   *R.S. Carpenter Collection*

Many of the 'Bulldog' class were given taper boilers by Churchward and this extended the life of a sizeable number into BR days. No. 3453 *Seagull* is coaled up for further duties at Croes Newydd on 24th April, 1949.   *R.S. Carpenter Collection*

Chapter Eleven

The 'New' 4-4-0s and Some Final 4-6-0s

Churchward had been one of those rare breed of engineers who believed in involving himself fully in the deliberations of his team. He frequently visited the drawing and other offices to see for himself how matters were progressing. In the drawing office he would perch at a draughtsman's board and ask pertinent questions, quite often brushing aside comments from the hovering chief draughtsman, preferring to hear the person concerned offer explanations or suggestions. This attitude of listening and discussing matters in hand earned him much respect from the draughtsmen - it made them realise that they had a say in the design process so often looked upon as the preserve of the CME or his immediate assistants. It most certainly ensured that all the team endeavoured to give of their best, to the benefit of the railway as a whole.

The foregoing was the underlying reason that the Swindon team produced so effective a set of locomotive designs when Collett took charge. The confidence and interchange engendered by Churchward's management approach had taken root amongst them and given them an excellent grounding in good design techniques. Had Collett been a leader of the calibre of his predecessor some very effective and advanced designs would eventually have resulted. But, for the early days of his incumbency, the Churchward designs were so advanced and so good that little needed doing in the way of more technological improvements. Collett fell back onto this, and, after the near catastrophy of the 0-6-2T, stuck firmly with his derivative approach to the Churchward programme. It worked quite well, but as time moved on the other CMEs elsewhere eventually began to overtake Swindon with their own designs. Maunsell, Stanier and Gresley all produced locomotives which began to match and surpass the now static technology on the GWR. Yet, despite this, there were some areas in which Collett did not place a restraining hand. One such example was the application of diesel power as we saw in the previous chapter. But, of course, the catalyst for that had been a request to consider diesels from the GWR Board. Collett sometimes bowed to commands from that quarter, eager to please them, but occasionally there was a hint of tongue-in-the-cheek, as we shall shortly see.

One little exercise which taxed the ingenuity of the drawing office was the design of a 'new' 4-4-0 in 1936 to satisfy a requirement for a light passenger tender locomotive for some of the branch lines which once comprised the old Cambrian Railways in Wales. Rather than design and build a new type, which would have been rather against the Swindon policy of moving away from four-coupled engines altogether, Collett took stock of the existing 4-4-0s still in service and, in a masterful directive, ordered that a hybrid design be schemed. This directive was sparked off by the fact that one example existed following a rebuild, which emanated by the chance of a 'Duke' and 'Bulldog' being placed on adjacent pits for major servicing. The 'Duke' frames were in very bad condition, sufficient to warrant scrapping of the engine, but the frames of the 'Bulldog' had plenty of life left. The 'Duke' boiler, cab, smokebox and fittings were therefore mounted on the

A further rebuild of the 'Dukes' by Churchward gave many of the survivors a Belpaire boiler.
No. 3267 *Cornishman* rests at Didcot in September 1934.   *R.S. Carpenter Collection*

One of the 'Dukedog' rebuilds of 1936/37, No. 9009 is found at Moat Lane in 1956, still
soldiering on.   *R.S. Carpenter Collection*

'Bulldog' frames to produce a versatile lightweight locomotive. There were a large number of old 'Bulldog' and 'Duke' class 4-4-0s due for withdrawal. Mechanically, many of these had several years of life left in them.

The frames and motion of a further 29 'Bulldogs' were fitted with the cabs and boilers from a similar number of 'Dukes' to produce what became quickly known as the 'Dukedog' class. Although these were decidedly Victorian in appearance with their out-dated double frames, they proved immediately successful and many lasted into the days of BR. They were also much cheaper to produce than any new design. Many of the 'Duke' boilers were satisfactory, after general repairs, for many more years' service. However, those beyond economic repair were replaced with new units, which were interchangeable with the originals.

Although keeping himself remote from the lower echelons of the design office, Charles Collett had, despite his outside preoccupation with matters psychical, retained his sense of humour. This was illustrated by his response to the often heard comments from some of the GWR Directors regarding the lack of their names appearing on some of the locomotives. Therefore this was remedied when the 'new' 4-4-0s appeared, with examples carrying the names of the most notorious of the complainers. These rather Victorian engines appeared in service and must have brought about some ribald comments from certain quarters, for after a short while it was decreed that such old-fashioned and insignificant engines did not warrant names! They were then removed and given to some of the 'Castle' class. Charles had made his point and no more was heard from the Board Room on such matters.

One particular event, in 1936, which blotted the copybook of the GWR, was the Shrivenham collision. This resulted in two deaths, the driver and one passenger, and was the first fatal train accident on the GWR since a collision at Reading in 1914. The locomotive involved was 'King' class No. 6007 *King William III*, which at first sight was classed as a write-off. Collett, however, had other views and after re-railing the wreck and towing it back to Swindon had it stripped down to the basic frames and inspected thoroughly. The impact of the collision had bent the front frame extensions backwards, the bogie was irreparable and the outer running plates very badly damaged. The boiler, however, was salvageable and what remained of the frames were optically checked for alignment and found to be out by only 0.012 inches. Rebuilding was most certainly possible, even though the locomotive was officially condemned. A replacement was in fact ordered, but the original was rebuilt to this order for accountancy reasons, apparently, and returned to traffic in a few months.

As the 1930s moved on with the United Kingdom clambering out of recession but the clouds of war gathering on the horizon, Charles Collett celebrated his 65th birthday by introducing a new class of mixed traffic 4-6-0. Retirement for him was not yet on the agenda, burying himself deep in the design of yet more locomotives seemed to be the best way to keep at bay his still deep feeling of the loss of Ethelwyn which continued to permeate his life. He was becoming more reclusive outside the office; he was also beginning to seek out some form of consolation by studying psychical and metaphysical documents. He was getting more involved in these spiritualist leanings, often going up to London for meetings. So far as

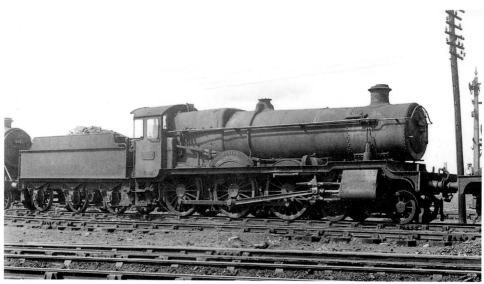

The 'Grange' class, totalling some 80 examples was basically a smaller-wheeled version of the 'Hall', and replaced withdrawn Churchward 2-6-0s. No. 6827 *Llanfrechfa Grange* sits idle at Bristol, 26th August, 1951.
R.S. Carpenter Collection

The 'Manor' was the Collett's final 4-6-0, only 30 being built. This example, piloting a 'King' on Dainton bank, is No. 7814 *Fringford Manor*, built in 1938 using parts from withdrawn 2-6-0s.
John Scott-Morgan Collection

holidays were concerned he took nothing but the odd half-day needed to attend these meetings. He had also, by now, become a strict vegetarian.

His health was still robust and there was much to occupy his mind with the new engines. He still clung resolutely to the Swindon moderate superheat philosophy, even though the other railways had for many years employed high-degree superheat. The locomotives were performing satisfactorily and coal quality was still high enough not to affect steaming performance, so why embark on a relatively expensive modification to high-degree superheat?

The need for a new locomotive stemmed from the requirement to replace the now ageing Churchward 2-6-0s of the '4300' class. The Running Department had been requesting a more powerful successor to that design for some years now as, quite often, these elderly 2-6-0s were being rostered for duties at the limits of their capabilities. A more powerful mixed-traffic type was needed of lighter weight than the 'Hall', having a wider route availability than that class.

The new 4-6-0 stemmed from Churchward's list of standard designs drawn up in 1901 (No. 2 in *Table 1, page 24*). This was for a two-cylinder locomotive with 5 ft 8 in. wheels and the standard No. 1 boiler. Collett resurrected this specification in the form of the '6800', or 'Grange' class. The only major changes to the original Churchward design were the adoption of the side window cab and screw reverse, otherwise in concept, the 'Granges' were pure Churchward. Costs were trimmed by utilising the wheels and motion from the pool of reconditioned items taken from withdrawn 2-6-0s. The first examples appeared in 1936 and a total of 80 were built up to 1939, when the war terminated what had intended to be the progressive replacement of all the 2-6-0s by the new 4-6-0s.

Upon introduction to service, the 'Granges' proved reliable and popular, providing the increase in power needed to cope with the traffic needs. They also had a good turn of speed, enabling them to be put onto passenger excursion and even some cross-country express work during peak traffic periods. However, there was one drawback, this being the axle loading of 18 tons restricting them from some of the branch and secondary lines over which the Moguls were acceptable. A lighter variant was needed.

Collett ordered that studies be undertaken to design a lightweight version of the 'Grange'. The obvious item to be dealt with was the boiler. None of the then existing standard boilers appeared suitable and a new one, to become the standard No. 14, was designed.

The 'Manor' class which stemmed from this study was to be Collett's last design for the GWR. The new boiler was not an immediate success, being a notoriously poor steamer from the outset, but by the time multiple complaints were being received, the 20 examples in service were left alone, for war had erupted and all research work was immediately curtailed. Nevertheless, the 'Manors' had their uses on the cross-country routes due to their substantial tractive effort compared to the 2-6-0s and 4-4-0s they replaced.

After the war, tests were carried out to pin down the cause of the poor steaming. This was traced to inadequate draughting, and as modifications were carried out a further batch of 10 was produced under the auspices of BR in 1950.

The 'Manor' signalled the closing of Charles Collett's design efforts for the GWR. As war approached and the country began to gather momentum in the

The 2-10-2T project, which never came to fruition.

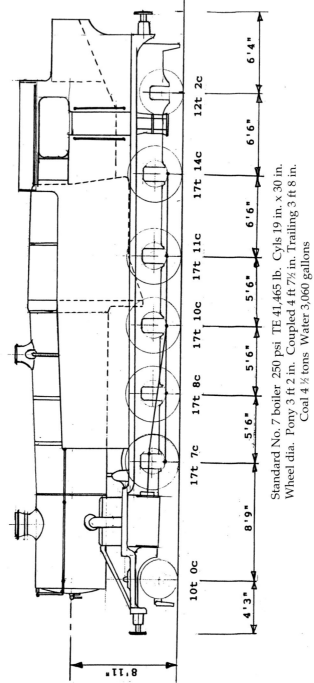

Standard No. 7 boiler 250 psi TE 41,465 lb. Cyls 19 in. x 30 in.
Wheel dia. Pony 3 ft 2 in. Coupled 4 ft 7½ in. Trailing 3 ft 8 in.
Coal 4 ½ tons Water 3,060 gallons

re-armament programme, emphasis on new developments sank to a low ebb. Soon the railways would be needed to serve the industries and armed forces as times changed. Production in the Swindon works was running at record levels never thought possible in the previous war, thanks to the Churchward and Collett expansion programme of the early 1920s which provided increased production space and, additionally, production techniques geared towards speedy and efficient assembly of locomotives now largely comprised of a range of standard parts. The legacy of all that planning carried out nearly 20 years earlier was to prove crucial in the years of conflict that lay ahead.

One interesting design study initiated by Collett in 1937 was for a massive 2-10-2T intended for the Ebbw Vale iron ore traffic, with its heavy trains, frequently double-headed and banked, struggling up grades of 1 in 58 to the steelworks. This locomotive would have employed the No. 7 boiler, so far only used on the 1919 47xx class 2-8-0. Coupled wheels were 4 ft 7 in. diameter and steam at 200 psi would have been supplied to two 19 inch diameter, 30 inch stroke, cylinders. The tractive effort of 41,465 lb. would have made it the most powerful tank engine in the UK. The gross weight of this leviathan, including four tons of coal and 3,060 gallons of water, would have been 109 tons 12 cwt.

Whether this design would have been a wise addition over South Wales lines abounding in curves is a relevant point, and may well have influenced matters with the Locomotive Committee. This proposal was never approved and remained a purely paper study. The double-heading plus banking of the heavy ore trains from Newport continued.

The management structure of the GWR had been destined to remain unchanged for the majority of Charles Collett's time as CME. The CME's department retained its independence from the other disciplines with the CME himself subservient only to the General Manager. Whilst other railways had been changing their management methods, Paddington and Swindon appeared content to continue in what was, essentially, a Victorian attitude of rather slow and, ultimately by more modern standards, inefficient management. The GWR Board was so imbued with their own past successes that advances elsewhere were to some extent ignored. In point of fact, the main reason for Sir Felix Pole's resignation back in 1929 stemmed from his inability to introduce the sorely needed management changes to eradicate the old-fashioned and well-worn methods of yesteryear. However, some inspirational requests did emanate from the Boardroom, a case in point being the introduction of diesel units for passenger work. So it was not all negativity.

Obviously, to change the way the railway was run was not on the agenda. The financial position of the GWR, as with all the railways, was getting progressively worse between the wars (*see Appendix Three*) and the added burden of increasing road competition from lorries, buses and private car compounded the adverse situation. The forthcoming war was to change the railway scenario in the UK dramatically and set the scene for Nationalisation which, this time round, was to become an accomplished fact.

Chapter Twelve

Electrification, War Again and Retirement

Although seemingly set on a path of continued steam traction for the main lines, the GWR did consider some electrification. The particular section which could have benefited from the adoption of electric traction was the main line west of Taunton.

In February of 1938 the Board of the GWR appointed Metz and McLellan, a firm of consulting engineers who had been associated with earlier studies of electrification, to prepare a scheme for the application of electric traction for the above section. This company had carried out many previous studies, notably for the Tyneside suburban scheme of 1904 and the North Eastern Railway's proposal to electrify its York to Newcastle main line. The resulting study for the GWR, dated February 1939, proposed an overhead wire system at 1,500 volts with four different types of locomotive; eight class 'I' 2,550hp of 1-Co-Co-1 arrangement, 40 class 'II' lower-powered variants of 2,100 hp, 55 class 'IIa' of 1,400 hp and 61 class 'III' Bo-Bo four axle types. The classes 'I', 'II' and 'IIa' were for main line work and the class 'III' for local trains, banking and shunting.

The superior performance of electrics at the lower speed ranges, particularly associated with higher starting acceleration and hill climbing, was shown to be beneficial on the steeply graded lines in Devon and Cornwall, However, all the changes to accommodate the scheme were written around the existing steam timetable. Electrification really shows great benefits if used on frequent train services of regular intervals rather than the intermittent demand called for by the existing operating conditions. Indeed, the relatively large number of locomotives listed above was as a direct result of providing adequate motive power in peak periods, such as when the summer holidays and Christmas services occurred.

The capital cost for implementing the scheme over a four year period, was quoted as being £4,361,100 and the associated saving in operating expenses was just £100,500 per year. The scheme therefore got no further than the report stage, but had it been decided to proceed, the onset of World War II would have terminated all work, as it did for the Southern Railway's brand new electric line from Motspur Park to Leatherhead which was terminated at Chessington South, at which station that line still finishes some 60 years on, despite much of the final section's civil engineering work being close to completion.

Collett was involved in the early talks associated with this electrification proposal but, as far as we know, did not set much store by it. His accelerating diesel railcar programme was of greater interest and, with more units entering service, was a cost-effective way in which to advance the branch, lightly used main line and cross-country services. Major main line advances would have to wait for the advent of diesel power in the 1950s and 1960s. Even then, the Western Region of British Railways selected diesel-hydraulic power in place of the diesel-electrics of the other Regions, such was the inbuilt independent thought process of Swindon under Nationalisation!

The apparent disinterest shown by the CME's department was not without foundation, as this electrification study was merely a repeat of the Weir Committee's 1931 report on 'Main Line Railway Electrification' so far as the GWR was concerned. What was at stake appeared to be a steady rise in the cost of coal throughout the 1930s as the collieries struggled to increase their profitability as the Country clambered out of recession. The impact of the study, which was quite widely publicised, was that coal prices moved down by 1s. 6d. per ton in April 1938 and stabilised at 23s. a ton by July. This drop was worth £250,000 a year off the GWR operating costs, no mean figure in those days. This drop far outweighed the savings estimated for the proposed electrification scheme.

Other railways, however did make progress with some electrification, in particular the LNER trans-Pennine Woodhead scheme, for which Gresley was engaging his design team in studies for electric locomotives aimed at freight and passenger operations. This programme actually did progress to the point where the first 1,870 hp locomotive was completed in 1941. Regrettably, Gresley never lived to see it.

One signal honour conferred on Charles Collett by Swindon Corporation was the naming of a new road after him. This took place in 1938, whilst he was still in office. Collett Avenue is to be found in the Rodbourne area of Swindon and runs parallel to Churchward Avenue in the same development.

As the inevitable war approached, the Ministry of Transport announced it would need locomotives for service overseas. The GWR had a large number of the popular 'Dean Goods' 0-6-0s approaching their retirement and 100 of these were selected from those in service and taken in for overhaul and conversion for their new role. Many of this class had served overseas in World War I and proved admirably suitable. They had a light axle loading, were simple designs and had a history of excellent reliability and so, rather than allot a similar number of the more modern '2251' class and latest version of the Mogul (there would have been insufficient of the former to fill the need), Collett ordered the drawing office to prepare diagrams for the modifications needed.

These modifications were wide-ranging, including air brakes, and pannier tanks complete with condensing gear amongst many. The latter were only actually fitted to 10 of the conversions. Due to the presence of other war work encroaching on Swindon, 20 of these conversions were contracted out to the Southern works at Eastleigh.

In mid-1939 the GWR received requests from Rolls-Royce in Derby and the Westland Company at Yeovil for the production of detail components associated with their growing war production needs. Collett refused absolutely to condone such work, going so far as to send a letter to the General Manager stating why such work could not be accommodated. He remembered all too well the disruption caused to his production schedules by munitions work during the previous war, when he was Works Manager.

Locomotives were being called in for maintenance ahead of their scheduled times in order the get the maximum number fully serviceable as war approached. Despite this, little or no overtime was being worked and Swindon was not at peak capacity, which created a bit of an undercurrent of annoyance amongst the workforce, as they knew that elsewhere plenty of overtime was being worked and earnings increased accordingly.

As war broke out Charles Collett was approaching 68 years of age and the spectre of retirement loomed. He was still in reasonably good health, but the increased pressures and responsibilities brought about by the impact of the war were, obviously, going to place a very heavy load on the CME and his staff. Swindon works, whilst keeping up its major overhaul and repair work, was not yet being prepared for large inroads of war work.

Continued pressure to take on war work was rejected by Collett. This refusal persisted until the knowledge of it reached Cabinet level. It is rumoured that M15 began to investigate Collett's background, but he got wind of this and began to prepare his arguments based on reports from World War I data which described the run-down in railway stock caused by munitions work interfering with the normal tasks. Eventually, pressure from the Board persuaded him to reverse his decisions. Such was the power a CME had in those days.

It was around this time that Charles bought a home in Wimbledon, where he would often stay on his London jaunts. Apparently, no one at Paddington knew of this address whilst he was still employed by the GWR, and only one or two select personnel at Swindon were told of it, and then only in strict confidence.

Throughout his life, Charles Collett, whilst eventually complying with demands to fulfil war-time needs, clearly did not like the prospect of military conflict or, that matter, blood sports. Exactly how much he was influenced on this, if at all, by his wife while she was alive we do not know. However, Ethelwyn has appeared as a gentle person, quite probably capable of persuading Charles to adopt a softer approach to what could often be harsh matters. As we have already seen, he appears to have been a person who, from early days, kept himself to himself, which probably led to some criticism of his attitude by those largely unaware of how much the loss of his wife affected him.

Although Collett had drifted out of ARLE proceedings in 1934, he clearly was involved in some meetings of the CME's Committee of the Railway Executive Committee during the early days of the war. This has been substantiated by a letter from Stanier to Gresley mentioning a meeting held on 29th February, 1940. At this meeting one topic of discussion was that of scrapping locomotives in a time of dire need for all available motive power, as Stanier wrote: 'CBC wanted to be different as usual, but we got him to agree on the scrapping of locos policy, on which you and I agree'. Clearly Stanier, with his previous experience of dealing with Collett, knew how best to argue the case and achieve a satisfactory outcome of a policy matter.

The last couple of years of Collett's time as CME were sprinkled with much time away in London, General Managers' meetings, Locomotive Committee meetings and, of course, the more frequent attendances at the psychical societies now so important to him. Design and administration matters were largely monitored by John Auld, who had been Assistant CME for nearly eight years now. By now, both Collett and Auld were well past the normal retirement age, Auld being the elder of the two. It has been said that Charles Collett persuaded Auld to stay on in order that he, Collett, could claim not to be the oldest at Swindon. There was also the story, from Collett, mentioned in Chapter Eight, that the Chairman had asked him to stay in office until he was 70.

Even though his mind was clearly active, Collett's talents were not being fully utilised for the benefit of the GWR. His influence on engineering matters at Paddington was, however, still very powerful, a feature he used to great advantage in providing explanations as to his gradual drift away from the CME responsibilities.

However, by the time the war was getting into its stride, Auld could no longer contemplate staying on, he was approaching 70, and categorically refused to continue beyond that age. This proved to be the catalyst which unseated Collett, who could not claim any longer not to be the oldest in service and he came to an agreement whereby both he and Auld would retire in the summer of 1941. A further reason to influence his decision was that the CME's policy, from 1941 to the end of the war, would be controlled by the Mechanical Engineer's Committee of the Railway Executive. He accordingly felt that such a body would demand considerable amounts of time on matters external to Swindon. There was also the the matter of switching large portions of the works to munitions, a matter which he had tried to resist for some time now. Whether or not his patriotism came in for adverse comment is not known, but every square foot of factory space that could assist the war effort was needed and the railways, despite their prime task of servicing and building locomotives and stock, were needed to provide extra manufacturing capacity. Events were, clearly, overtaking him and his outside interests were still very important so retirement it was to be.

All current production plans and associated orders were modified and large portions of the works were now turned over to wartime production. Anti-aircraft guns, barrage balloon gear and anti-aircraft predictors were all produced in quantity as the war gathered momentum. The Ministry of Aircraft Production placed contracts for the manufacture of the casings for 2,000 lb. bombs which soon became needed in vast quantities for the first squadrons of four-engined bombers being formed.

Some locomotive construction continued throughout the war, the emphasis being on freight types to cope with the huge need of motive power for the many extra trains conveying war supplies throughout the country. The Churchward 2-8-0 design had been revived in 1938 and orders placed for 53 to be delivered during 1940-42. Ten more 2-8-0 tanks were built in 1940 alongside a further 20 of Collett's '2251' class 0-6-0. Also produced were further batches of the '5700' class 0-6-0PT to cover the shunting and light freight needs of wartime. Additionally, the mixed-traffic fleet was still being enlarged, with batches of the 'Hall' class being constructed through the early war years.

In fact, Collett's anti-munitions stance mentioned earlier was, in the end, justified just before his retirement when an order from the Government for 80 Stanier 2-8-0s was placed on Swindon. This was on top of the orders for further batches of the '2800' class 2-8-0s already mentioned. The Ministry of Transport had worries that a shortage of freight locomotives would occur in wartime conditions already affecting the availability of stock. Swindon even received Ministry instructions that any war work which affected locomotive maintenance and construction should be contracted out. It appears that the lessons learnt from rather similar happenings in World War I had not been

2-8-0 No. 2893, a product of 1939, was only modified in the cab area by Collett. Here it approaches Salisbury with a sizeable freight in 1939 when nearly new.

R.S. Carpenter/Mace Collection

As war finished, some locomotives were converted to oil burning, with 20 examples of the Churchward 2-8-0s selected for the experiment. Here No. 4808 (formerly 2834) sits at Plymouth Laira awaiting eventual reconversion to coal, 8th August, 1948.   *R.S. Carpenter Collection*

heeded in the Ministry, which was all that Charles Collett had been trying to point out in the earlier days of the current war.

With development work now at a halt and the Swindon scene becoming more and more committed to its wartime programme, Charles Collett prepared to hand over his responsibilities as CME to F.W. Hawksworth who had been his Principal Assistant for some years now. July 1941 was to be the official transfer and Collett, as he approached his 70th birthday, appeared glad to be able to sit back and relax following a long and distinguished career of some 48 years on the GWR.

If there is a negative side to Collett's time as CME there is one particular feature of his design philosophy that needs mentioning at this stage. By 1912 Churchward had placed himself, and the GWR, about 10-15 years ahead of his contemporaries in the UK and could well afford to sit back and relax on the design side. Collett took most of the Churchward precepts to heart and his designs were to employ those well-tried ideas to excellent effect. However, the other CMEs were adopting the GWR design details on their own locomotives and applying their own further improvements to give their designs a gradual edge over those of Collett. That the GWR design philosophy could remain static was symptomatic of the inbuilt Swindon independence on such matters, being backed by the great advantages wrought by Churchward all those years previously. A case in point was that of superheating, with Collett steadfastly staying with the Swindon low to moderate degree whilst others had, for many years now, been utilising the now commonplace high degree type. So long as high grade coal was readily available at an economic price, the economy and performance of GWR locomotives was perfectly acceptable at their current level of superheating, But, clearly, should coal quality be affected, matters would suffer. Not only determined, from an early stage, to continue in office beyond the normal retirement age, Charles Collett was determined not to depart from those precepts so forcefully imposed by his predecessor.

As his career moved towards its close, Collett was absent from his office frequently. John Auld covered the ordinary day to day running of the CME's department. New design, as the war approached, was put mostly on one side apart from the occasional brief study. About the only new schemes which came to fruition were the later batches of diesel railcars and the updated 2-8-0.

He had, however, by following the Churchward standardisation policy, managed to bring about the simplification of the locomotive stock from the 17 types of 52 classes in 1921, to that of 13 types of 37 classes by 1941. This clearly had a considerable impact on maintenence costs which must have helped in the continual battle to maintain a reasonable working profit for the GWR. The current war effectively wiped out profit margins for the railways as a whole, as they struggled with the ever-increasing demands placed upon them. Never again were they to be the steady earner for their shareholders.

Little is known about Collett's retirement days, but he resigned his memberships of both the Civil and Mechanical Engineers Institutions almost immediately after retiring. Moving to the house in Wimbledon, he spent long periods of time delving into his obsessive passion for things psychical and metaphysical. He had for some time now been a member of the Institute of

Experimental Metaphysics, the Society for Psychical Research and the London Metaphysical Group. He lived on, through the war, to see the railways into Nationalisation and, with the steam locomotive still the prime means of power, passed away on 23rd August, 1952, a few weeks before his 81st birthday. His time had come to an end and he had, at last, achieved his desire of rejoining the one great love of his life, Ethelwyn. The small funeral attracted three notable figures, Frederick Hawksworth, Sir William Stanier and Sir Felix Pole, who paid their last respects to their colleague of those halcyon days at Swindon, when steam reigned supreme.

Just two years previously, no fewer than 50 of his designs, of five classes, had been produced by Swindon. Hawksworth had now retired and BR was busy inaugurating its programme of standard locomotive designs, most of which employed much of Swindon's technology. Charles must have entertained a quiet satisfaction in the knowledge of this continuation of his designs.

Of the Big Four, as the CMEs were frequently called in the inter-war post-Grouping years, only Sir William Stanier still lived on in retirement as a final connection with that time.

F.W. Hawksworth, in his time as CME.   *STEAM: Museum of the Great Western Railway*

Appendix One

Swindon Works - A Lesson in Productivity

In looking at the productive output of Swindon locomotive works so far as new or rebuilt locomotives are concerned, some interesting features are apparent. The analysis has been split into two distinct phases; firstly between 1902 and 1914, when Churchward was CME with Collett as Assistant Works Manager (1902-12), and Works Manager (1912-1919). Secondly, the period during which Collett was CME (1922-1941). It is to be seen that the productive output of new stock, in both cases, is cyclical. The war period (1914-18) is not included due to the extreme circumstances of the time, when a large part of the works was put over to the output of munitions.

1902-1914

Figure 1 shows the output in new locomotives per year. A 6-year cycle is evident between output peaks which, with the 'A' shop, recently built and covering some 5 acres, reached a maximum of 60 locomotives per year. The cyclical nature is probably a function of productivity being met by the improved workspace in the new shop at a better rate than before in the older, more cramped, facilities. Although such a cyclical pattern is not uncommon as progressive developments of an engineering design take place.

1922-1941

Figure 2 is illuminating, in that it shows a huge improvement in productive output made possible by the virtual doubling of the area of 'A' shop. This increase was made during 1919-21 at the end of Churchward's term as CME. He clearly saw the coming of the growth in rail travel as the country recovered after the war and lifestyles began to change. One matter which affected the population was the introduction, on a much wider scale, of paid holidays. The ordinary person could now contemplate a holiday away from home, and the railways were the obvious means of travel. Also, with the UK industries rebuilding and expanding to meet the needs of what was becoming a more affluent society, vast quantities of fuel and raw materials needed shifting. Additionally, many more people now needed to commute to work, jobs locally could no longer be guaranteed, and required the means of transporting labour forces to their place of work. The widespread ownership of the private car and the building of a road system to take it were yet to come.

As the older Victorian locomotives were progressively withdrawn and scrapped, Swindon busied itself building the modern replacements. Output slowly rose through to 1927, but was below the potential possible as recessionary pressures and their consequent squeeze on capital investment affected not only the GWR, but all the railways. However, there is one feature of the late 1920s and early 1930s timeframe, when the industrial recession affected the UK quite severely and the Government introduced schemes to finance the production rates needed to sustain the jobs in the struggling engineering industries. This was responsible for the amplification of the first cyclical peak of output in 1930. The downturn after this peak was mainly caused by the effects of the depression. From 1930 to 1933 the works was on short time, sometimes reduced to a three-day week for lengthy periods. 1932 was the worst year with only 65 new engines as against the 110 of only two years before. In point of fact a batch of 20 of the 2-8-0Ts built in the latter part of 1930 went straight into storage until being rebuilt as 2-8-2Ts in 1934.

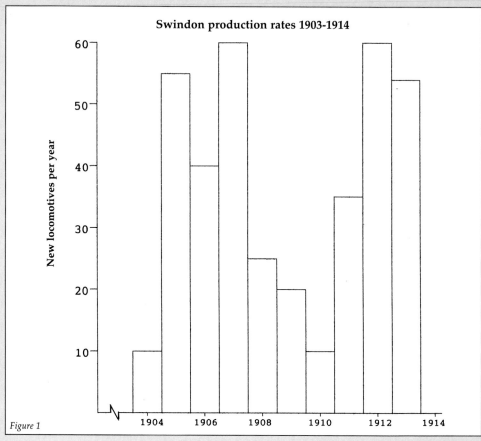

Figure 1

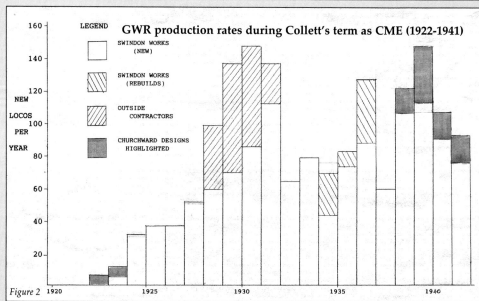

Figure 2

It is of interest to note that this first peak coincides with the greatest number of locomotives ordered from outside contractors. One might think that Swindon had reached its maximum possible output, but this peak, of course, was due to the encouragement of the railways by Government to place some of their orders outside of their own facilities. The maximum output it was not, for in 1940 Swindon works equalled this 1930 combined peak from its own resources. This peak indicates a 10-yearly cycle. The 1937 dip in productivity is interesting and almost certainly would be due to the shift of emphasis from the need to increase the express fleet to that of planning for more mixed-traffic locomotives for wartime needs in the light of threatening behaviour from Germany. It is noticeable that the last years, from 1939 to 1941, are associated entirely with the production of mixed-traffic and freight types which would be needed in large numbers in wartime.

The beginning of a tail-off in 1940-41 in the production rate is evident, but these figures are applicable to the building of GWR locomotives only. As the war progressed, munitions work increased, plus the building of some 'foreign' locomotives for the War Department, namely Stanier '8F' 2-8-0s, which incorporated many Swindon-inspired features and was the only locomotive of any type to be built by all the four main railways in addition to three of the major private builders.

Stanier 2-8-0, a Swindon-built example of 1943, displays typical wartime grime as it nears Goring troughs in 1943-4.   *John Scott-Morgan Collection*

Appendix Two

ATC on the GWR

One tends to forget, in these days, that for many years the GWR had an Automatic Train Control (ATC) system in operation. Much as this system was publicised, no other railway company was persuaded to adopt it (the Not Invented Here syndrome) until, in the late 1930s, Stanier began a programme of installation on the LMS. However, this was curtailed by the advent of the 1939-45 war.

Just how this ATC system grew is worthy of inclusion, for Charles Collett most certainly co-operated with the requests to improve the safety aspects of all types of rail traffic.

In 1906 the GWR installed the first ATC system on the Fairford branch, placing the test work under W.A. Stanier. This was purely for the purpose of assessing the feasibility of the system. The trials went well, and by 1910 more of the ATC system was equipping the main line between Reading and Paddington.

Initially, only a select few of the express locomotives were fitted with the equipment, which gave the driver an audible warning of the position of distant signals, a steam whistle if the signal was at danger and an electrically operated bell if it was clear.

In 1913 the danger aspect was improved whereby the brake vacuum was partially destroyed causing the brakes to start to come on. A siren sounded simultaneously. If the driver did not cancel the siren, the brakes were then fully applied to stop the train before the subsequent stop signal. Further trials proved the effectiveness of the enhanced system, but the advent of World War I prevented any more large-scale introduction of this pioneering application in the UK.

In 1923, Collett ordered that ATC become a standard fit on all top express locomotives. All the 'Castles' were built with it as standard and by 1927 all the older 'Stars' and 'Saints' were so fitted. In this latter year it was also decreed that all locomotives should have ATC installed as they were built or overhauled.

In 1930 the ATC-equipped track mileage was 372, but in that year a massive expansion was authorised, aided by Government grants to relieve unemployment, so that by September 1931 some 2,130 track miles were equipped. Fishguard was reached in 1937 and the final installation took place, at Penzance, in 1939. The engine crews were greatly pleased with this equipment, especially at night or in bad weather conditions when signal sighting was often difficult.

The fact that from 1921 to 1939 the GWR only had three passengers killed in accidents speaks for the efficiency of and wisdom in installing the ATC.

Appendix Three

GWR Financial Performance

It may be of interest briefly to analyse the financial ups and downs affecting the GWR during the years in which Charles Collett was at the top as CME. The data on the accompanying figure covers years between 1913 and 1938, with figures for the war years not available due to restrictions in force on such matters.

The large increase in income due to the inflationary effects brought about by World War I is clearly seen - about a two times increment between 1913 and 1921. The net profit, however, hardly changes as the expenses of wartime operations plus the inflation caused by the war soaked up much of the extra income. The effect of the 1926 General Strike and the 1930s depression are clearly visible, as are the effects on profits of these two events. The GWR did not ever have a chance to recover from these two body-blows and investment was starved, which accounts for the inability to update the motive power situation in the manner required and prolonging the life of steam locomotive developments. Much existing tooling and production methods were there due to the standardisation programme and, with capital expenditure restricted, it made sense to wring out all the cost advantages of that programme.

Even though the clear advantages of diesel power were there for all to see, the Swindon mentality was so wedded to the steam locomotive that acceptance of a radical change in motive power appeared difficult to get across - particularly to those whose lives were well steeped in steam technology.

So long as coal prices remained low, the steam locomotive was an economic means of power, but the events of World War II were to have a dramatic effect upon this fact, coupled with a quantum leap in propulsion technology.

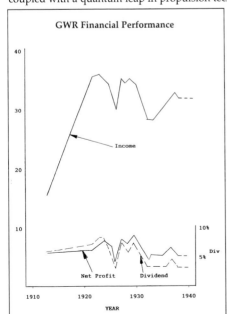

With the dividend down to the 3 per cent level from 1931, extra capital was not forthcoming and matters stagnated on the development side with only very selective programmes being approved by the Board. The same could be said for all the other UK railways and their decline as the prime mode of transport began to manifest itself, as the private car and road transport offered greater flexibility in both short and long haul situations.

It was against this background that Collett, in his last decade as CME, had to work and plan his production of new locomotives and stock to keep traffic flowing efficiently, in order to produce the best possible income upon which the continuation of the GWR depended. But, of course, World War II, with its dramatic effect upon railway operations and the accompanying Government control, destroyed all chance of funding the changes in both prime power and facilities' updates needed for continual modernisation.

Appendix Four

Collett Locomotives

Class	Type	Use	First Built	Subs Batch	No. Built Batches
4073 (Castle)	4-6-0	Express	1923	1924-50	179
4900 (Hall)	4-6-0	Mixed-Traffic	1924	1928-43	259
5600	0-6-2T	Mixed-Traffic	1924	1925-28	200
6000 (King)	4-6-0	Express	1927	1928-30	30
5700	0-6-0PT	Shunting/Goods	1929	1930-50	863
2251	0-6-0	Mixed-Traffic	1930	1934-48	120
5400	0-6-0PT	Passenger	1930	1931-35	25
6400/7400	0-6-0PT	Passenger	1932	1934-50	90
4800	0-4-2T	Passenger	1932	1933-36	95
7200*	2-8-2T	Freight	1934	1935-39	54
1366	0-6-0PT	Shunting	1934	-	6
6800 (Grange)	4-6-0	Mixed-Traffic	1936	1937-39	80
7800 (Manor)†	4-6-0	Mixed-Traffic	1938	1939-50	30
				Total	2,031

Notes:
* Rebuilt from existing Churchward '4200' class 2-8-0T and the earlier Collett class '5205' 2-8-0T.
† The first 20 of this class were rebuilds of the Churchward class '4300' 2-6-0.

Appendix Five

Other Collett builds of existing designs

Class	Type	Use	First Built	Subs Batch	No Built Batches
4700	2-8-0	Mixed-Traffic	1922-3	-	9
4300	2-6-0	Mixed-Traffic	1923	1925-32	50
5205	2-8-0T	Freight	1923	1924-40	105
4500	2-6-2T	Mixed-Traffic	1924	1927-29	100
5101	2-6-2T	Passenger	1929	1930-49	140
6100	2-6-2T	Passenger	1931	1932-35	70
9000*	4-4-0	Passenger	1936	-	30
8100†	2-6-2T	Passenger	1938	1939	10
3100#	2-6-2T	Passenger	1938	-	5
				Total	519

Notes:
* An amalgam of existing parts from the 'Bulldog' and 'Duke' classes of early 4-4-0s.
† Rebuilds of withdrawn Churchward class '5100'.
# Rebuilds of withdrawn Churchward class '3150'.

All other classes listed above, apart from the 'Bulldog'/'Duke' conversion ('9000' class) were, to all intents and purposes, standard Churchward designs with only minor modifications.

Appendix Six

Preserved Collett Locomotives

Type	Class	No.	Where based
4-6-0	King	6000	STEAM: Museum of the Great Western Railway, Swindon
		6023	Didcot Railway Centre
		6024	Didcot Railway Centre
4-6-0	Castle	4073	STEAM: Museum of the Great Western Railway, Swindon
		4079	Didcot Railway Centre
		5029	The Railway Age, Crewe
		5043	Birmingham Railway Museum, Tyseley
		5051	Didcot Railway Centre
		5080	Birmingham Railway Museum, Tyseley (for spares)
		7027	The Railway Age, Crewe
		7029	Birmingham Railway Museum, Tyseley
4-6-0	Hall	4920	South Devon Railway
		4930	Severn Valley Railway
		4936	Llangollen Railway
		4942	Didcot Railway Centre
		4953	Birmingham Railway Museum, Tyseley
		4965	Birmingham Railway Museum, Tyseley
		4979	Fleetwood, Lancs
		4983	Birmingham Railway Museum, Tyseley
		5900	Didcot Railway Centre
		5952	Cambrian Railway Society, Oswestry
		5967	Pontypool & Blaenavon Railway
		5972	Birmingham Railway Museum, Tyseley
4-6-0	Manor	7802	Severn Valley Railway
		7808	Didcot Railway Centre
		7812	Severn Valley Railway
		7819	Severn Valley Railway
		7820	West Somerset Railway
		7821	Great Central Railway
		7822	Llangollen Railway
		7827	Paignton and Dartmouth Steam Railway
		7828	West Somerset Railway
4-6-0	6959	6960	Gloucestershire Warwickshire Railway
		6984	Gloucestershire Warwickshire Railway
		6989	Buckinghamshire Railway Centre
		6990	Great Central Railway
		6998	Didcot Railway Centre
		7903	Swindon & Cricklade Railway
		7927	Wales Railway Centre, Cardiff
4-4-0	Dukedog	3217	Bluebell Railway
0-6-0	2251	3205	South Devon Railway

Type	Class	No.	Where based
2-8-2T	7200	7200	Buckinghamshire Railway Centre
		7202	Didcot Railway Centre
		7229	East Lancashire Railway
0-6-2T	5600	5619	Telford Steam Railway
		5637	East Somerset Railway
		5643	Lakeside & Haverthwaite Railway
		5668	Pontypool & Blaenavon Railway
		6619	North Yorkshire Moors Railway
		6695	Swanage Railway
		6697	Didcot Railway Centre
0-6-0PT	5700	3650	Didcot Railway Centre
		3738	Didcot Railway Centre
		4612	Bodmin & Wenford Railway
		5764 (L95)	Severn Valley Railway
		5775 (L89)	Keighley & Worth Valley Railway
		5786 (L92)	South Devon Railway
		7714	Severn Valley Railway
		7715 (L99)	Buckinghamshire Railway Centre
		7752	Gloucestershire Warwickshire Railway
		7754	Llangollen Railway
		7760 (L90)	Birmingham Railway Museum, Tyseley
		9600	Birmingham Railway Museum, Tyseley
		9629	Pontypool & Blaenavon Railway
		9642	Dean Forest Railway
		9681	Dean Forest Railway
		9682	North Norfolk Railway
0-6-0PT	6400	6412	West Somerset Railway
		6430	Llangollen Railway
		6435	Paignton & Dartmouth Steam Railway
0-6-0PT	1366	1369	South Devon Railway
0-4-2T	4800	1420 (4820)	South Devon Railway
		1442 (4842)	Tiverton Museum
		1450 (4850)	Gloucestershire Warwickshire Railway
		1466 (4866)	Didcot Railway Centre

An interior view of the engine shed at Didcot in 1998; it was built whilst Collett was in office and opened in 1932. The engine in the centre is No. 6998 *Burton Agnes Hall*. Other Collett locomotives visible include 'Manor' No. 7808, '5600' No. 6697 and 'Hall' No. 5900. Odd man out is Wantage Tramway's No. 5.

P.G. Barnes

Appendix Seven

Preserved Churchward designs
as built by Collett

Type	Class	Number	Where based
2-8-0	2800	2885	Formerly at Southall Railway Centre
		3802	Bodmin & Wenford Railway
		3803	South Devon Railway
		3814	North Yorkshire Moors Railway
		3822	Didcot Railway Centre
		3845	Swindon & Cricklade Railway
		3850	West Somerset Railway
		3855	Pontypool & Blaenavon Railway
		3862	Northampton & Lamport Railway
2-6-0	4300	5322	Didcot Railway Centre
		9303 (7325)	Severn Valley Railway
2-8-0T	5205	5224	Churnet Valley Railway
		5227	Wales Railway Centre
		5239	Paignton and Dartmouth Steam Railway
2-6-2T	5100	4110	Swindon Railway Works
		4121	Birmingham Railway Museum, Tyseley
		4141	Llangollen Railway
		4144	Didcot Railway Centre
		4150	Severn Valley Railway
		4160	West Somerset Railway
		5164	Severn Valley Railway
		5193	West Somerset Railway
		5196	?
		5199	Llangollen Railway
2-6-2T	6100	6106	Didcot Railway Centre
2-6-2T	4500	4555	Paignton and Dartmouth Steam Railway
		4561	West Somerset Railway
		4566	Severn Valley Railway
2-6-2T	4575	4588	Paignton and Dartmouth Steam Railway
		5521	Swindon Railway Works
		5526	South Devon Railway
		5532	Lllangollen Railway
		5538	?
		5539	Wales Railway Centre, Cardiff
		5541	Dean Forest Railway
		5542	West Somerset Railway
		5552	Bodmin & Wenford Railway
		5553	Birmingham Railway Museum, Tyseley
		5572	Didcot Railway Centre

Bibliography

A History of the GWR - P. Semmens, George Allen & Unwin
Air Mails of the British Isles - H. Stanley Redgrave, privately published and printed
An Outline of G.W. Locomotive Practice, 1837-1947 - H. Holcroft, Locomotive Publishing Co.
Archives, Merchant Taylors' School
ARLE Minutes (notes on) - compiled by Geoffrey Hughes
British Locomotives of the 20th Century - O.S. Nock, PSL
Churchward Locomotives - B. Haresnape & A. Swain, Ian Allan
Collett and Hawksworth Locomotives - B. Haresnape, Ian Allan
Experiments With Steam - Charles Fryer, PSL
Felix J.C.Pole, His Book - Sir Felix Pole, Town & Country Press
Great Western Express Passenger Locomotives - Martin Smith, Argus Books
Great Western Locomotive Design, a Critical Appreciation - Revd J.C. Gibson, David & Charles
Great Western Saints and Sinners - W.A. Tuplin, George Allen & Unwin
GWR Two-cylinder 4-6-0s and 2-6-0s - Rodger Bradley, David and Charles
Grime and Glory - Tales of the GWR 1892-1947 - Adrian Vaughan, Alan Sutton
Historic Railway Disasters - O.S. Nock, BCA
Institution of Civil Engineers, Archives
Locomotive Adventure - H. Holcroft, Ian Allan
Locomotive Engineers of the GWR - D. Griffiths, PSL
Master Builders of Steam - H.A.V. Bulleid, Ian Allan
Proceedings of the Institution of Civil Engineers
Proceedings of the Institution of Mechanical Engineers
Rails in the Valleys - J. Page, Guild Publishing
Railway Air Services - John Stroud, Ian Allan
Richard Maunsell, an Engineering Biography - J.E. Chacksfield, Oakwood Press
Royal Trains - Patrick Kingston, Guild Publishing
Sir Henry Fowler, a Versatile Life - J.E. Chacksfield, Oakwood Press
Sir William Stanier, an Engineering Biography - O.S. Nock, Ian Allan
Sir William Stanier, a New Biography - J.E. Chacksfield, Oakwood Press
Stanier Locomotives - B. Haresnape, Ian Allan
Swindon Steam, 1921-51 - K.J. Cook, Ian Allan
Swindon - The Legacy of a Railway Town - J. Cottell and K. Falconer, HMSO
The Churchward 2-6-0s - David Andrews, Line One
The Collett Saga - Margaret Chadd, Elvery Dowers Publications
The Great Western at Swindon Works - Alan S. Peck, OPC
The Great Western at Work 1921-1938 - Adrian Vaughan, PSL
The Great Western Railway, a New History - Frank Booker, David & Charles
The Great Western Railway Magazine
The Four Great Railways - M.K. Bonavia, David & Charles
The GWR - 150 Glorious Years - P. Whitehouse & D. St John Thomas, David & Charles
The GWR Stars, Castles and Kings - O.S. Nock, David & Charles
The Illustrated History of Railways in Great Britain - G. Freeman Allen, Marshall Cavendish

Index

Numbers in **bold** type refer to illustrations.

159